DIVINELY DISABLED

A 30-DAY DEVOTIONAL
to Discovering God's Heart for the Disability Community

Nadia Ibrahim Mossburg

Ink & Willow

INK & WILLOW
An imprint of the Penguin Random House Christian Publishing Group
A division of Penguin Random House LLC
1745 Broadway, New York, NY 10019
inkandwillow.com
penguinrandomhouse.com

Italics in Scripture quotations reflect the author's added emphasis.

An Ink & Willow Trade Paperback Original

Trade Paperback ISBN 979-8-217-15205-6
Ebook ISBN 979-8-217-15206-3

Editor: Leslie Calhoun
Production editor: Joyce Wong
Designer: Nicole Block
Production: Louisa Francavilla
Copy editor: Eldes Tran
Proofreaders: Surina Jain, Alissa Fitzgerald

Printed in Malaysia

9 8 7 6 5 4 3 2 1

First Edition

The authorized representative in the EU for product safety and compliance is Penguin Random House Ireland, Morrison Chambers, 32 Nassau Street, Dublin D02 YH68, Ireland. https://eu-contact.penguin.ie.

For details on special quantity discounts for bulk purchases, contact specialmarketscms@penguinrandomhouse.com.

In loving memory of

my dad, Shawki S. Ibrahim, who always encouraged
me to write—and kept waiting for my first book.

And, to my mom, Katy G. Ibrahim, as well as the rest of my
family: Mathew, Asher, and all the guys; the London-based
Liebats, and the California-based Ibrahims—
for their unwavering love and support along the way.

I love you all.

Contents

Enjoying Hidden Oases: Embracing Uniqueness and Cultivating Joy

Traveling with Others: The Importance of Fellowship

Beyond the Horizon: Living Purposefully, Dreaming Boldly

INTRODUCTION

Preparing for the Journey

AT SOME POINT IN YOUR LIFE, DISABILITY WILL TOUCH YOUR STORY. You may be thinking, *Are you sure?* But there's no doubt in my mind, friend. Consider whether you or someone you know fits one or more of the following descriptions:

- **DEMONSTRATES A PATTERN** of social avoidance that exceeds normal shyness
- **STRUGGLES WITH FOCUS** and organization, to a greater extent than simply being "disorganized"
- **NEEDS A DARKENED ROOM** and/or frequent breaks due to a health condition
- **EXPERIENCES DIFFICULTIES HEARING** and/or often asks others to repeat themselves
- **IS IN RECOVERY** for misusing or abusing alcohol and/or over-the-counter medication, prescriptions, or illegal substances

- **IS CURRENTLY UNDERGOING** (or has undergone) cancer treatment that affects their ability to complete daily tasks and/or impacts their physical and mental wellness

- **LIVES WITH A CHRONIC CONDITION** or a short- or long-term disability

- **CARES FOR AND/OR SUPPORTS** someone with an illness, injury, or disability

A "yes" to any of the above statements means disability has been woven into your story. If it hasn't yet, chances are it will be. Disability transcends age, race, gender, education, income, and employment status. Some are born with disabilities, while others acquire them through illness, injury, or aging. Wherever you find yourself today, please know you are not alone.*

When I was about twelve, the reality of living with a lifelong disability hit me like a freight train. I remember thinking, *Why do I have cerebral palsy (CP)? Why am I one of the 1 in 4 people with a disability in the United States and the 1 in 345 children born with CP?*[1]

If you're not familiar with CP, it is a central nervous system condition. It affects my brain's messages to my muscles. The nature and severity of CP vary depending on several factors, including the extent of the brain injury in a young child and/or length of time the brain goes without oxygen. My type, known as spastic CP, is the most common and results from damage to the cerebral cortex (the brain's motor area). Muscle tightness, joint stiffness, and jerky movements characterize the condition. In my case, it affects all four limbs and is not typically painful. Although I require assistance with daily activities,[2] I'm fairly independent once in my power wheelchair.

* Some in the disability community prefer people-first language (people with disabilities), while others see their disability as a primary aspect of their identity (disabled people). I use the two interchangeably, as is common for professionals in the disability community.

Disability Statistics

Globally, one billion people—more than fifteen percent of the population—live with a disability, representing the world's largest minority group.[3] Only five to ten percent "of the world's disabled are effectively reached with the gospel, making disability community one of the largest unreached—some say underreached—or hidden groups in the world."[4]

In the United States, more than seventy million (one in four) people live with a disability.[5] The difficulties they encounter contribute to significantly higher rates of mental health distress, making finding hope and healing essential.[6] While faith has proven to be a powerful force for positive mental health,[7] the intersection of faith and disability often remains fragmented and incompletely explored.

Living with a disability or chronic illness profoundly impacts all aspects of life. Beyond the physical limitations, emotional distress, and social isolation, people may face additional challenges, including navigating public conversations and adapting to new circumstances. Spiritual questions often arise amid these experiences: *If God is so loving and powerful, why did this happen to me? Will my life ever be "normal" again?* These questions can leave individuals feeling lost and alone.

Even if you are not personally living with a disability, you may be one of the millions of Americans dedicated to caring for loved ones with disabilities or chronic illnesses. A 2023 Guardian Life Insurance Company of America report indicates that 100 million Americans provide care to family members with disabilities.[8] Additionally, U.S. Bureau of Labor Statistics data show that 37.1 million people provided unpaid eldercare in 2021–22.[9]

Directly caring for or even watching a loved one struggle with affliction can be physically, emotionally, and spiritually draining. You may have your own questions and challenges: *Why did this happen to them and not me? What is this journey going to look like for them and me? How will it impact our relationship? And how am I going to hold it together?* These questions can often consume our hearts and minds.

Caregiver stressors may include feelings of isolation, fear, and uncertainty about the future, balancing caregiving with other responsibilities, and dealing with prolonged financial strain due to lost wages coupled with the cost of care. The cumulative toll of caregiving can lead to anxiety, depression, and even substance abuse. Given these multifaceted complexities, many wonder where to turn for help and support.

Disability and Faith

When it comes to an issue like disability, even church leaders, pastors, and counselors committed to building inclusive communities may be unsure where to begin. Author and pastor Lamar Hardwick in his book, *Disability and the Church*, "estimates that 80 to 85 percent of churches [worldwide] don't have any level of special-needs ministry."[10]

According to the international ministry Joni and Friends, church leaders can often feel overwhelmed by the prospect of providing ministry to those with disabilities, given the broad range of disabilities and the lack of experience or knowledge. "For church leaders who have not interacted much with someone who has a disability, 'disability' can seem foreign, alien, and (to be perfectly honest) somewhat frightening."[11] A 2014 study of Bible college and seminary leaders revealed the majority of those surveyed believed their graduates were "not at all (3.4%) or only a little (70.7%) prepared to respond to spiritual and theological questions resulting from disability-related human experiences."[12]

Statistics, although somewhat dated and sparse, suggest that people with disabilities may feel unwelcome or unable to participate fully in faith communities, despite the fact some may practice spiritual disciplines (e.g., prayer, Bible study, fasting, etc.) more often than their nondisabled peers. For example:

- **32.3% OF FAMILIES** affected by disabilities say they have left a church, because their child is unwelcome or excluded.[13]

- **46.6% OF PARENTS** of disabled children say they avoid religious activities, because their child is unwelcome or excluded.[14]
- **DISABLED PEOPLE** are less likely to attend religious services than their nondisabled peers. For example, a survey found 45% of adults with disabilities attend church monthly, compared with 57% of adults without disabilities.[15]
- **DISABLED PEOPLE** are 28% more likely than their nondisabled peers to describe religion as unimportant in their lives.[16]
- **PEOPLE WITH** hearing, physical, and emotional disabilities are more likely to pray several times a day than the rest of the public.[17]

A growing number of denominations and parachurch ministries are offering resources and training to assist churches in becoming more accessible to and inclusive of disabled people. More Bible colleges and seminaries are offering courses, minors, or certificates in disability ministry. Still, there is a consensus among experts that more can and should be done to advance the belonging of people with disabilities in the church.

My Story

My spiritual growth and acceptance of my disability have been anything but a quick, easy, or linear process. Although I grew up in a home where faith was not practiced, the Lord graciously began tugging at my heart at the age of twelve through the kindness and joy of my camp counselor, Carol. When I was sixteen, Karen, my aide in high school, began sharing Scripture with me in response to my many questions. Two years later, I put my trust in Jesus and his work on the cross for me.

In the last thirty-seven years, I've accepted the reality that my relationship with disability—like any relationship—has its ups and downs. Some days, I'm filled with faith that God has used and is using all things for my good and his glory. I'm content despite my limitations, and I'm thankful God continues to work in and through my life in unexpected ways. On the not-so-good days, questions and doubts crowd out the Truth and scream for my attention. I'm discontent, questioning where and how God is working—and longing for Jesus's return.

When I was thirty, I faced another crossroads. I'd responded to the Lord's leading me to pursue a second master's degree. As part of a related internship program, I spent the summer of 2001 working in Washington, DC. This life-changing experience gave me the opportunity to meet countless people living—not simply existing—with disabilities. They held key roles, made notable workplace contributions, lived independently, and had families. This profoundly impacted me, given my previous experience at a large, private-sector company where I was one of only two employees with a visible, physical disability.

I slowly began to believe that a life and career in Washington, DC, were possible for me. I traveled to and from work using public transportation. I went shopping, to the movies, and out to eat with other interns. While I still needed assistance transferring from my wheelchair to the bed or toilet, my newfound freedom and independence brought a mindset shift. Yes, I was born with a disability. It varied from the "norm," but it was not "bad" or "special." It was simply a fact. I realized the real "problem" usually stemmed not from me as a person, but from the surrounding environment and attitudes. I went from complete dependence in the Midwest to independence in Washington, DC, with support at certain times.

This perspective differed somewhat—and still does—from what I heard and experienced both inside and outside the church. Responses to my disability in various faith communities over the years have ranged from complete acceptance to patronizing. I have developed genuine friendships, but there are also those who—even after years of knowing me—only feel comfortable making a bad joke about my power wheelchair driving skills. Over the years, friends have patiently prayed and happily stepped in to practically help me. Yet, others have attributed unanswered prayers for healing to my lack of faith and patience. Some have shared, with a plastered smile and a pat on my arm, that watching me navigate life's daily activities inspires them.

Many friends and colleagues with disabilities possess an immediate and distinct disdain for characterizing their ordinary lives and behaviors as "inspiring" or "inspirational." They insist they are simply living out the life laid before them. There's nothing extraordinary or special about it. In fact, they believe such responses hold an underlying negative connotation: A disabled person offers little else than inspiration and gratefulness for the nondisabled, who are thankful for what they *don't have*, as if living with a disability is one of life's most terrible tragedies.

Some experience a visceral reaction to even the slightest hint of ablest language and attitudes, while others—intentionally or unintentionally—seem to disregard any nuanced language. Truth be told, my reaction to ablest language and attitudes typically falls somewhere in the middle. Sometimes I can hold my tongue; other times my tongue overpowers even my most earnest attempts at self-control. Any willingness to extend grace to those unfamiliar or uncomfortable with disability is evidence of the Lord's unending patience and unrelenting yet gentle reminders that my identity as a child of God supersedes all other identities I cling to, including that of disability advocate. I appreciate that not everyone holds this perspective. I also recognize that not everyone has been exposed to disability to the same degree. So, for some, the idea that those of us with disabilities are not "special" remains a foreign concept.

I recall Karen, my high school aide, saying to me, "The church is made up of imperfect people who don't always reflect God's heart." This wisdom has been pivotal in helping me extend grace in the most uncomfortable situations. Still, some situations have required the involvement of church leadership. These encounters have taught me that sometimes "shaking the dust off my feet and moving on" is the only appropriate response.

Jesus and Your Story

When the daily struggles, critical remarks, and reactions of others feel overwhelming, you and I can turn to Scripture's truths—words divinely inspired and written by people who endured shipwrecks, illnesses, and even death. These writers understood perseverance in the midst of difficulty.

But there is no greater example of a life of suffering than the one lived by Jesus himself. His life and death exemplify profound hardship, unwavering perseverance, and resilience. He faced everything from rejection in his hometown to the ultimate betrayal by Judas Iscariot, one of his disciples. He also experienced the full spectrum of human emotions. He wept at the death of his friend Lazarus and expressed righteous anger when the temple was desecrated into a marketplace.

He endured the brutal physical torment of flogging and crucifixion.†

Jesus had forewarned his disciples, "In the world you will have tribulation. But take heart; I have overcome the world" (John 16:33). Even his closest followers, who had witnessed countless miracles, grappled with doubt and fear despite this advance warning of opposition. Therefore, if you find yourself wrestling with grief or questions, or feeling crushed by adversity, know that you are in good company. Such struggles are a natural part of the human experience, even as we hold the deep conviction that this life is not the end.

We will all face troubles, sorrow, and pain this side of Heaven: "For we do not wrestle against flesh and blood, but against the rulers, against the authorities, against the cosmic powers over this present darkness, against the spiritual forces of evil in the heavenly places" (Ephesians 6:12). As children of God, we are caught in the enemy's crosshairs, where adversity and affliction are often the unfortunate consequences.

In John 16, as Jesus was foretelling his death and resurrection,

† Medical experts confirm the immense suffering Jesus likely endured as he went to and hung on the cross, including shock, cardiac stress, dislocated shoulders, exposed veins and bones, and the agonizing inability to exhale.

he said to the disciples, "So also you have sorrow now, but I will see you again, and your hearts will rejoice, and no one will take your joy from you" (John 16:22). Jesus's death and the disciples' hardships were not the end of the story.

Friends, the same holds true for us. Our tears of sadness and anguish will one day be wiped away, and we will be with him.

In the meantime, while we wait for God's full healing, I pray God speaks to your heart through each of the reflections as we journey through this book together. My hope is that the prayers offer time for a holy pause—to feel his nearness and comfort. I trust that God will give you a glimpse of the beautiful mosaic of grace he is creating through what seem like the broken pieces of your story. And that you will gain courage to take the next steps.

I hope this book serves as a catalyst for biblical conversations about disability. The reflections serve merely as a starting point. I encourage you to delve into the Share Your Story section at the end of each day. There, you'll find questions and prompts designed to promote spiritual growth and practical action. If you're looking for resources to help along the way, check out my website at www.divinelydisabled.com, which includes national organizations, agencies, and programs that provide practical assistance to individuals with disabilities, their families, and churches.

Whether you are grappling with a disability yourself and wondering if God has good plans for you, or whether you're walking with someone feeling that way, thank you for coming alongside me to learn and to grow. Thank you for giving yourself space to explore some difficult topics and emotions. I know firsthand that navigating disability can be daunting at times. But let's remember we are not alone. Jesus is with you and me—and he will see us through.

Entering the Wilderness

Finding Your Way

DAY 1

Facing Unseen Opposition

FIGHTING HIDDEN BATTLES

I am weary with my moaning;
every night I flood my bed with tears;
I drench my couch with my weeping.
My eye wastes away because of grief.

Psalm 6:6–7

AS A YOUNG CHILD, I developed the hypothesis that my disability would disappear by age thirteen. My reasoning and support for this still elude me. When my hypothesis proved invalid (surprising, I know), I plummeted into utter despair, feeling like I had no one to talk to. My tight-knit family had an unspoken rule on faith and hard emotions: These two topics were generally off-limits.

My mom and dad came from different faith backgrounds. Rather than force my older sister, younger brother, and me to practice a particular faith, my parents felt strongly that we should each choose which faith to live by if or when we were ready. So, we chose, as a family, to avoid the topic.

When it came to my disability, my parents—both immigrants from war-torn Middle Eastern countries—approached it as they did every other challenge: with an unwieldy amount of grit, strength, and determination. They unequivocally embraced the hard reality that my physical therapist had shared several years earlier: I would navigate the world using a wheelchair rather than walking. If this news was at all devastating, my siblings and I witnessed no evidence of it as young children.

But the older I got, the more intensely I wrestled with the reality of my disability. Rather than talk about my feelings, I ignored them. It's not surprising they ultimately emerged as sarcasm and anger. From ages twelve through sixteen, this internal struggle nearly led me to end my life. (If you find yourself struggling in this way, I encourage you to reach out to a family member, friend, pastor, or counselor.) Little did I know that God had surrounded me during that time with Christians who were praying for my salvation.

Looking back, I felt similar to the author of Psalm 6. He said, "I am weary with moaning; every night I flood my bed with tears; I drench my couch with my weeping."

Maybe you have been there, or maybe you are there right now. If so, you are not alone. You might think, *That's an easy thing to say,* but I promise: It's more than a pithy platitude.

Psalms 6 and 56 paint a wonderful picture of a God who is near to the broken-hearted and fiercely protective of his children, sending enemies fleeing in terror (Psalms 6:10; 56:9). He is compassionate, feeling both sorrow for your difficulties and empathy for your pain. He hears your weeping (Psalm 6:8) and pleas, and he accepts your prayers (Psalm 6:9). He counts your tossings and is close enough to capture your tears in a bottle (Psalm 56:8).

You may find it strange that God would keep track of the most painful and challenging moments of your life—oftentimes the very experiences you would prefer to forget. But Revelations 21:4 says, "He will wipe away every tear from their eyes, and death shall be no more, neither shall there be mourning, nor crying, nor pain anymore." He keeps a record, because one day he will make all things right: He will replace every ounce of sorrow with infinitely more joy.

Your secret battles fought on this side of Heaven are shadows of the larger, unseen spiritual battle taking place. Ephesians 6:12 says,

"For we do not wrestle against flesh and blood, but against the rulers, against the authorities, against the cosmic powers over this present darkness, against the spiritual forces of evil in the heavenly places." Notice that Ephesians 6 does not call into question the wrestling but rather clarifies with whom you wrestle. You might, like me, find this truth nearly impossible to remember and apply when you're facing hardships. The reality is it can be far easier (and more emotionally satisfying) to direct anger, frustration, disappointment, and sadness toward those closest to you rather than unseen, evil spiritual forces "in heavenly places."

So, what can you do when the source of your struggle is completely outside your realm and authority? First recognize that you were never meant to manage the struggle on your own, then ask God to take it. As your protective, loving Father, he will exact justice for sadness caused or wrong inflicted on you, his child. You may not witness this justice on this side of heaven, but rest assured your Father will not let a single harmful or painful act of the enemy go unvindicated.

LORD, *thank you that nothing is hidden from you, and you want it that way. We don't have to be hesitant about bringing our deepest sadness or fears to you, because you already know them all. How comforting to know that you keep a record of our most painful moments, not because you find pleasure in our affliction, but so one day every tear can be wiped away. Please help me see you as my loving, compassionate, and caring Father even on my most difficult days. And give me your grace to extend that love and compassion to those closest to me, even when I struggle to accept their assistance.*

IN JESUS'S NAME, *Amen.*

Share Your Story

PROMPT: What battles have you been reluctant to share with others because you're afraid of what they may think?

ACTION STEP: Identify at least two resources that address this type of struggle, even if they do not provide a disability perspective. Consider reaching out to someone to talk. If you do not feel comfortable talking to a family member, friend, or church leader, reach out to a mental health or similar service provider in your area. They are often required to maintain confidentiality. One option is the 988 Lifeline, which is available by calling, texting, or chatting. The judgment-free conversation is kept confidential.

FOR LOVED ONES AND CAREGIVERS: Describe at least one personal struggle you have when it comes to supporting your loved one or client with a disability or chronic illness. Explore ways to connect the loved one or client with community, so the weight of support is shared.

FOR PASTORS AND CHURCH LEADERS: Develop a list of individuals in your church family who may be willing and able to provide practical support for people facing difficulty. What are some ways this type of support could be incorporated into existing ministries?

DAY 2

Forlorn but Not Forsaken

GOD SEES YOU

As he passed by, he saw a man blind from birth.

John 9:1

I'VE OFTEN FELT more isolated and lonely even after spending weeks around people. For me, these feelings especially surfaced following my husband's rotator cuff surgery. Several post-surgical complications left him in constant pain, which meant I needed to rely on personal care assistants (PCAs) for all my daily activities—from getting up to going to bed and everything in between. My days seemed packed and divided between working remotely and being assisted by a PCA, with little time for much else. My reliance on PCAs also required schedule adjustments for me that limited my ability to spend time with Mathew, meet up with friends, and even attend church.

This monumental shift impacted me more than I anticipated, given Mathew had been my primary caregiver since we married in 2018. I had enjoyed a certain level of flexibility and freedom with Mathew, and we had become accustomed to spending much of our days together. But in the days and weeks following his surgery, that time together was reduced dramatically.

Researchers agree that isolation and feelings of disconnectedness occur more frequently for those touched by disability—either as a person with a disability or a caregiver. The reasons vary but may include the nature of your disability and need for assistance or accommodation. For example, more frequent medical care or a lack of accessibility might mean you miss opportunities to connect with others. Also, those without disabilities may be hesitant to engage, especially if they have little to no experience with disability. It's best in these situations to let others know what they can expect and what you prefer: "My assistant will be with me, but don't hesitate to stop by and visit."

Although the disabled experience loneliness more often than their peers, its impact certainly extends well beyond the disability community. One study found that of respondents between the ages of eighteen and forty-four, nearly fifty-three percent reported being lonely often. And in 2023—for the first time in history—the U.S. Surgeon General identified loneliness as a public health concern, dedicating a report to the issue. We were created to be seen, and when we don't feel seen, it can affect our health.

In his book *How to Know a Person: The Art of Seeing Others Deeply and Being Deeply Seen*, *New York Times* opinion columnist David Brooks explored how effective communication contributes to meaningful connection. He believes the following conversation skills make all the difference:[18]

- ACTIVELY LISTENING rather than multitasking,
- ELIMINATING THE URGE to compare by bringing up your own similar experiences,
- BEING COMFORTABLE with reflective pauses, and
- ASKING QUESTIONS to gather more detail.

Friend, if you are struggling with loneliness and feeling unseen, take a closer look with me at the opening verse of John 9: "As he passed by, he saw the man blind from birth."

Despite everything Jesus had endured, he was fully present and empathetic to those in need around him. He *saw* the blind man.

Scripture doesn't provide details about everything taking place in and around Jesus as he walked by the man. Given that the Sabbath prohibited work, we can safely assume things were quiet. But Jesus's acknowledgment of the disabled man was noticeable. So much so that the disciples, who were with Jesus, began questioning him about the man's situation. Despite their questions, Jesus reached out to the blind man for connection, and in doing so, helped him experience the importance of connection as well.

While Bible commentaries don't say much about it, the verse itself says so much about Jesus.

Just a few verses earlier, he was on the verge of being stoned. In John 8, after he confronted the scribes and Pharisees over their pride and response to the woman caught in adultery, the Jews accused Jesus of being "a Samaritan" and "hav[ing] a demon." This was no offhanded comment, but a direct attack. Tensions were high between the Jews and the Samaritans. The Samaritans considered themselves to be Israel's true descendants and saw Jerusalem's temple as illegitimate. So, the Jews intended to pierce Jesus with their sharp accusations. Angry and offended by Jesus's proclamations about himself (and his exposure of their sin), "they picked up stones to throw at him, but Jesus hid himself and went out of the temple" (John 8:59).

We don't have to endure a pointed attack to struggle or become jaded or upset. Sometimes the daily disability-related challenges we face can lead to bitterness, anxiety, and self-focus, which research shows can affect physical, emotional, and psychological well-being. We can easily and quickly let self-pity overcome us.

Jesus's response in chapters 8 and 9 showed no hint of such a response to hardships. Matthew Henry, a seventeenth-century Bible commentator, provided this perspective on Jesus's response to the man in John 9: "Though the Jews had so basely abused him, both by word and deed gave him the highest provocation imaginable, yet he did not miss any opportunity of doing good among them."[19]

You may be thinking, *Yes, but he is Jesus . . . the Holy God who is wholly human. I don't have it in me.* I agree completely. It is inherently impossible for us to achieve this on our own. But, as 2 Corinthians 1:3–4 says, "Blessed be the God and Father of our Lord Jesus Christ, the Father of mercies and God of all comfort, who comforts us in all our affliction, so that we may be able to comfort those who are in any affliction, with the comfort with which we ourselves are comforted by God." Whether support, reassurance, or relief come through interactions with others or time with God, Scripture reminds us that God himself is the source of all comfort.

I love Matthew Henry's additional comment on this seemingly simple verse in John 9: "And if we know or apprehend anything of Christ, it is because we were first known of him." Amen. Whether no one sees or everyone sees, God saw first. He saw before the foundations of the world, before you were even formed in our mothers' wombs. He not only saw but still sees—and cares to see—into the deepest parts of our lives and souls. He knows us, and because of that, we can know him.

LORD, *thank you for your sacrifice on the cross. In that moment, you were forsaken by the Father. And, in that same moment, we as your children never had to worry about or fear being alone again. When I feel forgotten and alone, remind me that you are with me. You see me, know me, and understand me. Help me remember that you will never see me as an outsider simply because of my limitations. Give me love for and patience with those who question my ability to contribute or serve. Help me share your comfort with others facing difficulties.*

IN JESUS'S NAME, *Amen.*

Share Your Story

PROMPT: Describe a time when you felt unseen or unheard. What feelings or emotions surfaced in that situation? Describe your response. In what way has that experience impacted your response in subsequent similar encounters? How have these encounters helped you be even more sensitive to the needs of others who face feelings of loneliness and isolation?

ACTION STEP: Write a note to yourself thinking through how you could change your response to feeling lonely or isolated. Consider how you could change your response to others dealing with similar feelings.

FOR LOVED ONES AND CAREGIVERS: As a caregiver or loved one of someone facing a disability, in what ways—if any—do you feel unseen or unheard in your current role? What impact has it had on you? How has it shaped your perspective on caregiving? How might it help you extend compassion and grace to other caregivers?

FOR PASTORS AND CHURCH LEADERS: As you consider those in your church family facing a disability or hardship, describe any efforts to ensure the individual and their loved ones feel less isolated or lonely. Describe the success and subsequent impact of these efforts. What, if any, additional steps could be taken?

DAY 3

Calling for Help

SEEKING ANSWERS IN THE DARKNESS

But he knows the way that I take; when he has tried me,
I shall come out as gold.

Job 23:10

THE SCHOOL CAFETERIA, transformed with crepe paper and colored lights for dances, held a bittersweet magic for me. My sister, Lila, and my friends had decided I needed to regularly participate in school dances, a quintessential aspect of junior high and high school. The absence of accessible transportation meant keeping my power wheelchair at home, but that hindered no one. They spun my manual wheelchair in circles, popped wheelies, and swayed my chair to the eighties music. Those moments became and have remained some of my most cherished, vivid memories of growing up.

Yet, without exception, a familiar shadow would creep into my mind at some point in the evening and persistently whisper, *Why me? Lord, isn't there something you can do to change my situation? Please help me be able to dance and move like everyone else.* The shadow would surface during fast-paced songs as my attempts to emulate my friends' movements would result in jerky and off-beat motions.

Slow songs struck my frail heart even more acutely. During these songs, I observed from the dance floor's dimly lit edge as students paired off and gently swayed together. In these moments, sadness mixed with a yearning to simply *move* washed over me. Despite my friends' efforts to include me, a sense of otherness would invariably surface. After all, they were navigating the dance floor with ease, and I wanted to do the same.

Whether you've had a disability since birth or acquired one later in life as a result of an illness or injury, you have likely asked, *Why did this happen? And why did this happen to me? Why didn't you answer my prayers, God?* This age-old question of *Why?* has existed for centuries: *Why is there evil, pain, sadness, and disease? If God is so good, why doesn't he intervene? If he could raise Lazarus from the dead, why didn't he heal my mom?* Sometimes our family, friends, and other supporters are the ones looking for answers: "If you had only . . ." or "If she'd just . . ."

Research shows that, when faced with difficulty, pain, and/or uncertainty, your mind naturally looks for an explanation or resolution. Your brain naturally wants answers and not getting them negatively affects you. Think about it: How many times have unresolved questions caused you to speculate and worry? This not only consumes mental energy but also triggers the fight or flight response. The increased stress and anxiety often leave you feeling tired and overwhelmed.

To alleviate this discomfort, your brain resorts to a degree of problem-solving that ranges anywhere from simply acknowledging the uncertainty and seeking answers to creating your own rationale, even if inaccurate or unhelpful. And unfortunately, fabricating your own answers can lead to negative thinking patterns and irrational beliefs.

Throughout Scripture, we see people asking "Why?" and making assumptions about what they need to do or what God is doing (or not doing) in the face of uncertainty. In the early chapters of Job, Job's friends insisted that his sin and need for repentance had led to his trials and tribulations (e.g., losing his children, enduring sickness and health issues, etc.). But Job believed that if he could only find God and present his case, God would hear him, act justly, and change his circumstances.

We, too, can sometimes fall into the trap of thinking that change can only come through specific prayers or actions. In Habakkuk 1:1–3, the prophet Habakkuk asked God to move. He said, "O Lord, how long shall I cry for help, and you will not hear? . . . Why do you make me see iniquity, and why do you idly look at wrong?" Even Jesus's disciples sought an explanation for the man who had been born blind. They asked in John 9:2, "Rabbi, who sinned, this man or his parents, that he was born blind?"

Yet God's responses often defy our expectations. Habakkuk 1:5 reminds us, "Look among the nations, and see; wonder and be astounded. For I am doing a work in your days that you would not believe if told." Even if God allowed us to see his plans, the wonder and creativity of his ways would be incomprehensible. His plans would still exceed our wildest dreams. His ways and plans are good, because he is the embodiment of good.

This truth applies even when we consider disability. In John 9:3, Jesus explained that suffering served a higher purpose: "It was not that this man sinned, or his parents, but that the works of God might be displayed in him." That work includes making us more like Jesus and displaying his glory in and through us, even when it's difficult to see, understand, or accept. In other words, we must choose to believe God's promises and trust God's character, even when everything around us feels and screams otherwise.

Job displayed this type of faith in Job 23:10, when he declared, "But he knows the way that I take; when he has tried me, I shall come out as gold." No conceit or pride underscored Job's declaration. He did not see himself as more holy than his friends. Rather, he trusted in God's good purposes, in God's intimate knowledge of him, and in God's justice and judgment. He believed God could see the true nature of his faith and character. And Job trusted that God would look beyond outward appearances to judge his heart authentically.

Trials and difficulties often strengthen our faith while exposing areas where our hearts might be resting in something other than God. Maybe it's your career, a relationship, or your education. Whatever it is, sometimes being at the end of our rope is exactly where God wants us.

Former pastor turned surfer Britt Merrick explained life's difficult seasons this way: "[W]e want answers, we want clarity—but God wants our trust. . . . [A]nd rather than answers (which he does not promise), he wants to give us himself (which he has promised)."[20]

LORD, *the darkness feels suffocating, and I'm not even sure what to pray. Please help me. I don't know what to do. Thank you that in such moments the Holy Spirit intercedes for me. My heart and mind want to know why, but—honestly—knowing the answer wouldn't take away the hurt and the pain. Thank you that Psalm 34:18 reminds me that you are close when I face trials. Use these circumstances and trials in my life to draw me closer to you—and to bring you much glory.*

IN JESUS'S NAME, *Amen.*

Share Your Story

PROMPT: What thoughts and feelings emerge as you consider an area of your life where unanswered questions linger? How could having answers to these questions change your feelings and/or emotions?

ACTION STEP: Based on these feelings, find and record in a digital note or a journal at least two Scriptures that address or capture your emotions. Ask God what he wants to show you. Here are a few suggestions:

- **ANGER:** Ephesians 4:26–27; James 1:19–20; Proverbs 29:11
- **LOSS AND DESPAIR:** Ecclesiastes 1:2; Lamentations 3:19–20; Luke 19:41–44; Matthew 23:37–39
- **UNCERTAINTY:** Psalm 23:4; Isaiah 41:10; Philippians 4:6–7; Jeremiah 29:11; Matthew 6:31–34

FOR LOVED ONES AND CAREGIVERS: How do your loved one's or client's emotions and/or feelings affect you? Consider how to create space for a dialogue on this topic, and identify at least three strategies to protect your own psychological and emotional health.

FOR PASTORS AND CHURCH LEADERS: Many believers tie their trust in God to specific outcomes. Identify several strategies you could use to encourage your church family to focus on God's unwavering character rather than on circumstances and outcomes.

DAY 4

When Hopes Go Unfulfilled

UNMET EXPECTATIONS

For freedom Christ has set us free; stand firm therefore, and do not submit again to a yoke of slavery.

Galatians 5:1

AS I MINGLED WITH OTHERS at the fall community outreach event that had brought together several local churches, an older gentleman who served on the intercessory prayer team asked me, "Can I pray for your healing?"

The minute the simple question left his lips, I felt my heart begin to race and my palms begin to sweat. I frantically looked around for my husband, Mathew, who was talking with a friend a few feet away. (Mathew occasionally doubles as my bodyguard when well-meaning strangers target me to test their prayer skills.) I tried to clue Mathew in by making eye contact with him, but the crowds rendered me helpless.

"Um, I . . ." I hesitantly responded, not wanting to offend the man or seem ungrateful. "I appreciate the sentiment, but I've made peace with God. I believe God can . . ."

Before I could finish my thought, Mathew appeared and politely, but firmly, declined the request. As we walked away, the man mumbled under his breath about my lack of faith and my need to repent.

In my thirty-seven years of following Jesus, strangers have approached me countless times asking whether they could pray for my healing. Often these instances have been followed by condescending reminders of my need to trust God and possess more faith. For so many years, I wrestled with discouragement and shame following such encounters, convinced that something in me hindered God's ability to heal me.

Following one such incident nearly ten years ago, my pastor reassured me the strength of my faith should not be in question. He characterized this behavior by strangers as spiritual abuse. Until then, I had never considered such a perspective, but I now recognize the accuracy and validity of his description.

Maybe you or someone you know has had a similar experience.

Today, the term "ableism" is used to refer to discrimination toward people with disabilities. In the ableist view, a disabled person is fundamentally "less than," flawed, and must be "fixed." This particularly troubling perspective on disability suggests that salvation only comes through Christ's sacrifice plus physical healing. Ableism in the church

Recognizing Spiritual Abuse

In 2 Corinthians 1:24 (NLT), the apostle Paul makes references to inappropriate behavior in the church at Corinth. He says, "But that does not mean we want to dominate you by telling you how to put your faith into practice. We want to work together with you so you will be full of joy, for it is by your own faith that you stand firm." He makes a distinction between controlling behavior and biblical correction, reiterating that salvation comes through faith alone.

This passage suggests church leaders should not dictate how members put their faith into practice. By today's standards, doing so may be considered spiritual abuse. This type of abuse uses coercive and controlling behavior in the context of faith communities and teachings. Like other forms of abuse, spiritual abuse can be physical, sexual, or emotional in nature.

shows up in many different ways, including deciding on worthiness and blessings based on outward appearance. It wrongly attributes disability to a lack of faith, the presence of underlying sin, or a generational curse.

Some disability and faith experts believe that the church's willingness to accept disability must, as a prerequisite, accept human frailty beyond the theoretical or broad sense. The church must look disability in the eye and surrender fully to the sovereignty, grace, and wisdom of God, being at peace with God's unique design for each of his children.

But in addition to this heart shift, the disability community can help by being willing to educate and hold the church accountable, with the same firmness, grace, and patience that Paul demonstrated with the teachers in Galatia. Professor Thomas E. Reynolds explains, "In the absence of preconceived expectations fueled by dominant visions of what is 'normal,' people with disabilities can convey a powerful sense of personhood and dignity and offer many gifts to their communities."[21]

LORD, *thank you that in the body of Christ, we are one. Thank you that your work is not based on our disability status. In you, we are forgiven and free by the blood of Jesus. Lord, where there is a lack of knowledge around disability issues, please give me the grace and wisdom to respond with patience. I pray for opportunities to help educate my brothers and sisters in Christ. Where there is ableism, please expose it. I ask for your wisdom, guidance, and protection as I engage in sharing information on this topic. I want to maintain as much unity as possible in the body of Christ but not be afraid to speak up against ableism and other forms of discrimination. Lord, please use any conversations on this topic to bring your body closer together. Open up opportunities for me and other people with disabilities to share their gifts with the church.*

IN JESUS'S NAME, *Amen.*

Share Your Story

PROMPT: Have you or someone you know experienced ableism? If so, describe the circumstances and how it was handled.

ACTION STEP: Honestly examine your current church experience. What recommendations can you provide leadership related to ableism? If a past encounter with ableism is keeping you from attending church, consider what it would take for you to return to church.

FOR LOVED ONES AND CAREGIVERS: Have you been present when someone else has experienced ableism? Describe how the situation was handled and share any lessons learned.

FOR PASTORS AND CHURCH LEADERS: How have you or would you address ableism from members of your congregation? What changes, if any, have you seen as a result? If you were to add a statement on the church website that stated your church's position on ableism and other forms of discrimination, what would it include?

DAY 5

Wrestling with Blame

WHO IS AT FAULT?

The man said, "The woman whom you gave to be with me, she gave me fruit of the tree, and I ate." Then the Lord God said to the woman, "What is this that you have done?" The woman said, "The serpent deceived me, and I ate."

Genesis 3:12–13

MY HUSBAND MATHEW'S LOVE for Jesus and his care, kindness, and genuine humility are some of his many character qualities I'm drawn to. Even in the early days of our relationship, it was evident to me that difficult and painful experiences had positively shaped his faith and understanding of God's character.

While we were dating, I learned that, after a period of sobriety, Mathew had relapsed while being treated for a broken leg. Around the same time, a car accident left one of his family members permanently disabled. The combination of circumstances and prescribed pain medication left him wanting to take a "drug holiday," as he often explains when sharing his story. This led to homelessness for Mathew: a season characterized by deep despair and nearly life-ending blame.

For months, Mathew replayed in his mind the devastating series of events. Ruminating on his mistakes as well as others' accusations against him pulled him into a psychological black hole he couldn't escape on his own. A state-appointed counselor ultimately intervened on Mathew's behalf. The counselor admitted him into a mental health facility for seventy-two hours, then insisted he complete a drug rehabilitation program. Following treatment, he entered a sober living home and attended a men's retreat.

As he has frequently shared when telling his story, "It was there [at the retreat] that I heard God say to me, 'How arrogant and prideful of you to think that my sacrifice is not sufficient to cover your sins.'" That night, he humbly prayed Psalm 86:5 (NLT): "O Lord, you are so good, so ready to forgive, so full of unfailing love for all who ask for your help." As Mathew explained, "That prayer marked the beginning of an ongoing journey for me: one to see myself as a loved child of God, completely forgiven and free, because of Jesus's sacrifice on the cross for me, personally."

You might, like Mathew, carry the burden of self-blame for past decisions. Perhaps you've been unjustly blamed for circumstances beyond your control. You may even blame God for your disability.

As a defense mechanism, blame protects your ego and helps you avoid uncomfortable emotions. Not surprisingly, blame often appears as you endure and process difficult and painful situations. Reactions to blame include acceptance and accountability, blame shifting, clarifying misunderstandings, or a total lack of response. A response to blame depends on several factors, including where blame is directed (either at ourselves, others, or the Lord). At times, blame may be shifted from the person responsible to an innocent bystander.

Blame isn't only a modern-day response to life's hardships. Scripture passages throughout the Bible confirm that the use of blame as a defense mechanism has existed for centuries—masking guilt and fear (Genesis 3:10), grief (John 11:21), anger (Joshua 22:15–18), and helplessness (Numbers 20:5).

In Genesis 3:12–13, we read, "The man said, 'The woman whom you gave to be with me, she gave me fruit of the tree, and I ate.' Then the Lord God said to the woman, 'What is this that you have done?'

The woman said, 'The serpent deceived me, and I ate.'" When questioned by God, fear led Adam to blame Eve, and Eve to blame the serpent. They had each in some way defied God's authority and instruction. This story serves as a reminder that God alone is able to rightly judge a situation. Subsequently, Adam, Eve, and the serpent suffered distinct consequences for their actions.

Blame masked grief in the story of Lazarus (John 11:21). Lazarus's sisters sent word to Jesus that their brother was sick. Rather than immediately going to Lazarus, Jesus stayed where he was two days longer. Without the detail of John 11:4 (that the illness would not cause Lazarus to die, but rather result in God's glory), you could easily begin to question his wisdom and care for his friend. From Martha's limited perspective, her response seemed appropriate: "Martha said to Jesus, 'Lord if you had been here, my brother would not have died.'" Martha loved Jesus and had witnessed miracles, yet she could not see beyond the circumstances in front of her.

Can you, like me, relate to Martha? We too can jump to conclusions informed by grief and disappointment when Jesus doesn't respond in the way we expect. Amid heartache and pain, we can easily travel down the "if only" trail, which some in the addiction recovery community refer to as the "enemy's playground." But holding on to blame hardens our hearts, creates wedges in our relationships, and plants seeds of bitterness and anger in our souls. Understanding and appropriately dealing with blame is the only way we can take the first step toward healing.

If you're unsure how to move forward out of a blaming cycle, prayerfully consider the suggestions below. As you work through blame, you also may want to consider seeking support from a trained counselor or mental health professional.

- ACCEPT GOD'S UNDERSTANDING AND GRACE. Recognize your inability to be good on your own, to change the past, or to control others' behavior. Prayerfully take responsibility for your part in the situation. Others must also accept responsibility for their actions, but you must recognize that you can't control their behavior. Seek wisdom from the Lord through prayer. Ask other mature believers for their perspectives but avoid gossip or slander. Pray for discernment about what you might need to change versus what you should accept as part of his good plan for you.

FOCUS ON SOLUTIONS AND PERSONAL GROWTH. Move from blame toward actively pursuing solutions. While it's important to acknowledge pain, avoid rumination. Consider next steps related to your personal growth. Be realistic, understand your own limitations, evaluate your current capacity, and establish clear boundaries for your own mental and physical health.

EMBRACE FORGIVENESS AND SEEK SUPPORT. Scripture reminds us to cast our burdens on the Lord, because he cares (1 Peter 5:7). Pursue supportive friendships. For areas where you hold systematic blame, pursue established avenues for peaceful resolution. Ask the Holy Spirit for wisdom and strength to forgive. Use your experiences to inform your advocacy efforts and facilitate change where possible.

PRACTICE QUIETNESS AND TRUST. Pray for God's peace. Focus on your own spiritual growth and pray for opportunities to assist others facing similar challenges. Trust the Lord to protect and vindicate you. Repent for the ways you've tried to exact justice on your own. Balance reflection with acceptance, surrendering to God's will. Focus on the present, trusting God's good plans. Rest in the Lord's love, acceptance, and forgiveness. Remember: He is your defender.

LORD, *where I've let blame take up more space in my heart than I should, please forgive me. I need your help letting go of the anger and bitterness toward those who have caused me harm and difficulty. Help me fix my eyes on you. Open my eyes as I study your character. When I struggle, bring to mind the truth that you took my guilt and shame and paid the penalty for my sin. Give me eyes to see and a heart to accept your mercy and grace in my life. Thank you for not giving me what I deserve and, instead, giving me what I don't deserve. Lord, help me take a step forward today, trusting that you will use everything in my life for your glory.*

IN JESUS'S NAME, *Amen.*

Share Your Story

PROMPT: In what areas of your life does blame show up? Does it mask as an emotion (e.g., joy, sadness, surprise, fear, anger, disgust) or a feeling? If so, which one and why do you think that is?

ACTION STEP: Set aside a few minutes in your day. Ask the Holy Spirit to show you where you need to replace blame with the Lord's forgiveness. Make note of these areas either on your phone or a piece of paper. Then, if you have put your trust in Jesus's sacrifice, write "Forgiven by God" over each item. You may extend the same forgiveness to others. If you're not there yet, that's okay. Ask God to reveal himself to you. (Given the nature of this step, it may be helpful to involve a trained professional.)

FOR LOVED ONES AND CAREGIVERS: Journal about the ways blame shows up in your life and how it impacts your relationship with your loved one or client. How does it impact other relationships? Is there one particular area or situation where you've had difficulty letting go of blame? If so, based on the suggested steps above, identify at least one step that can help you move forward.

FOR PASTORS AND CHURCH LEADERS: How can you more effectively equip those in your congregation who face disability (or painful and difficult circumstances) to navigate self-blame, blame toward others, or blame toward God in a compassionate, biblical manner?

Dawn of a New Day

Seeing Glimmers of Light

DAY 6

All Hope Is Not Lost

RECOGNIZING DIVINE PRESENCE

And their eyes were opened, and they recognized him. And he vanished from their sight.

Luke 24:31

EVEN IN THE YEARS FOLLOWING the passage of the Americans with Disabilities Act (ADA), meaningful employment remained a significant challenge for many, a reality that persists even today.

My own early career mirrored this complex reality. I desperately wanted a job that utilized my writing and editing skills. I also hoped for a position that afforded me financial independence and the ability to work alongside my nondisabled peers. So, without reservation, I accepted my first and only job offer as an indexer at a major publishing company.

Despite a few unresolved logistical details, I remained optimistic as I began this new chapter. God's past provision gave me faith that he would provide once again. He eventually removed most of the initial hurdles, until the only one left was the lack of sufficient weekend help. So, for two and a half years, I traveled to my parents' home every weekend. When that arrangement proved less than desirable, I ultimately resigned myself to moving back in with my parents and commuting to the office several days per week.

However, other challenges had less obvious solutions. Because of my single-digit typing speed, some colleagues refused to work with me. Additionally, timed proficiency tests significantly influenced advancement decisions, and leadership was reluctant to allow me more time. I soon felt my publishing career—a symbol of longed-for independence—slipping away before it had truly begun. In this period of profound disappointment, I wondered, *God, where are you?*

If your circumstances take an unexpected twist like mine did, you might question whether you've taken a wrong turn on your life's path. When you experience pain or a hoped-for dream doesn't materialize, joy can quickly morph into despair and skepticism. These unwelcome companions on your faith journey can erode your trust and confidence in God, making it difficult to see the divine path before you.

In Luke 24, Cleopas and his companion walked a remarkably similar road. Shattered expectations weighed heavily on their hearts and souls. They had listened to and followed Jesus's teachings and had even beheld his power. But then, they witnessed Jesus's crucifixion. Although some women spoke of his resurrection, their words seemed unbelievable.

And then a stranger joined Cleopas and his companion on their walk.

We know from the text that Jesus intentionally prevented the two disciples from recognizing him. You might wonder why, in such a moment of despair and disillusionment, Jesus chose not to reveal his identity. Although the text doesn't give a definitive answer, it does provide five principles you can hold on to when God feels distant and hidden:

- **REMEMBER THAT GOD SHOWS UP IN LIFE'S ORDINARY MOMENTS.** We can so easily and subtly assume the Lord will move or answer our prayers in a particular way. When our circumstances turn out differently than expected, we can become jaded. Unmet expectations can lead to anger, bitterness, sadness, and resentment. There is no place this seems more likely than in our relationship with God. In the immediate aftermath of the crucifixion, Jesus drew near to the disciples in a surprising manner.

The reality is, however, that he may reveal himself in unexpected ways. Galatians 5:22–23 reminds us that the Holy Spirit's presence and work can show up as "love, joy, peace, patience, kindness, goodness, faithfulness, gentleness [and] self-control." The manifestation of one or more of this "fruit of the Spirit" may be evidence of God's nearness.

DO NOT MISTAKE AN INABILITY TO RECOGNIZE GOD'S PRESENCE IN YOUR LIFE AS HIS ABSENCE OR LACK OF CARE. Like the disciples, we can so often draw conclusions about God based on our limited knowledge or experience. The truth is he is an all-knowing, ever-present, and all-powerful God and Father. Scripture offers repeated assurances that God's presence is constant, and his care unwavering. He promises never to leave us nor forsake us.

ASK THE HOLY SPIRIT FOR HELP IN UNDERSTANDING SCRIPTURE, THEN BE OPEN TO HIS GUIDANCE. When the disciples struggled to draw connections between the Old Testament and current events, Jesus responded with patient instruction. Just as he patiently led the disciples to a deeper understanding, he accompanies us on our journey, revealing truth in his own time.

ALLOW GOD TO TRANSFORM YOUR HEART THROUGH A PERSONAL RELATIONSHIP. God wants to grow our experiential knowledge of him. He longs to have a relationship with each of us characterized by a transformed heart. Consider how Jesus deliberately "acted as if he were going farther" (Luke 24:28). He seemed to be assessing the sincerity of the invitation from Cleopas and his companion, because he sought genuine connection rather than simple recognition.

INVITE JESUS AND OTHERS INTO YOUR LIFE. The pivotal moment of recognition for the disciples occurred during an intimate act—a shared meal when Jesus took bread, gave thanks, broke it, and offered some to them, which was reminiscent of the Last Supper with the disciples prior to his crucifixion.

"[M]eals hold significant spiritual, cultural, and communal importance. They are often depicted as moments of fellowship, covenant, and divine provision. Throughout Scripture, meals serve as settings for teaching, worship, and the demonstration of God's faithfulness."[22] This portion of the story also alludes to another important principle: that of inviting Jesus into the personal and significant spaces of our lives regardless of how we feel. We are also reminded that we are not meant to live life in isolation but rather actively pursue fellowship with other believers (Luke 28:29).

LORD, *thank you that you are a friend who sticks closer than a brother. Your patience with us is unmatched. Help me look back on my life with eyes of faith to see all the ways you've carried me and cared for me in my darkest hours. I want to believe you will do the same now. Please bring people who I can talk to across my path. Thank you that this season of darkness will not last forever. Help me to trust you, even when I can't see what is ahead. Strengthen my heart. Give me eyes of faith to recognize your hands orchestrating all that is loving, joyful, peaceful, kind, and gentle.*

IN JESUS'S NAME, *Amen.*

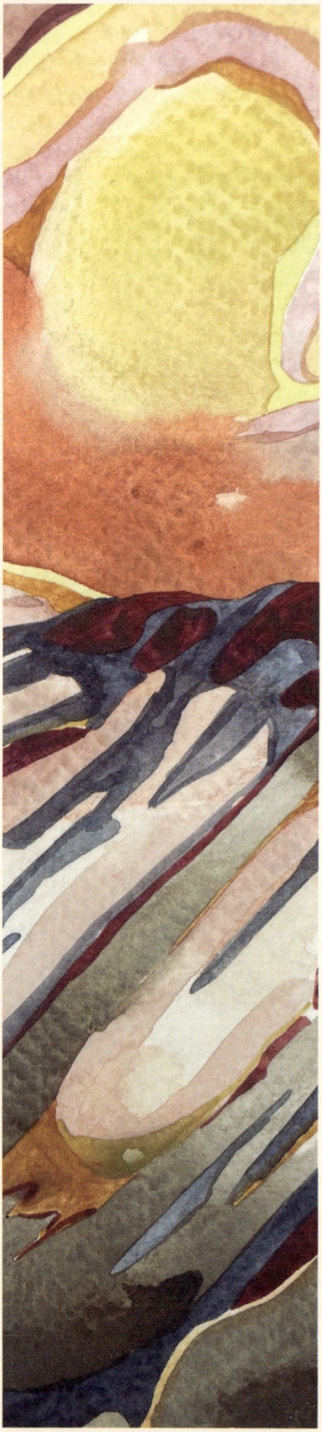

Share Your Story

PROMPT: Our actions and words say a lot about the condition of our hearts. Where in your life do you see evidence of the Holy Spirit (divine presence)? In what areas can you invite the Lord to do more? Keep in mind that the Spirit may not manifest in the manner you expect.

ACTION STEP: Take time to thank the Lord and the people around you for the ways you have been blessed by them. Send thank you notes or make phone calls as you feel led. Ask the Lord to show you if there are additional ways you can bless others.

FOR LOVED ONES AND CAREGIVERS: Being tired or overworked can steal your joy and hinder your ability to see the good around you. If you find yourself in that place today, what might help to create an atmosphere conducive to renewing your mind and spirit? If necessary, ask others for help in creating space and time to recall all the ways God has encouraged or blessed you over the last few days.

FOR PASTORS AND CHURCH LEADERS: In accordance with Galatians 5:22–23, what are some ways that leadership in the church can encourage and support those facing difficulty, hardship, or disability? It may be as simple as extending grace and patience to individuals facing hardship who seek prayer on a regular basis. Keep in mind that this does not need to be an organized ministry or large-scale effort.

DAY 7

Become Like a Child

EXPERIENCING PEACE IN WEAKNESS

Let the little children come to me and do not hinder them, for to such belongs the kingdom of heaven.

Matthew 19:14

SEVERAL YEARS AGO, I attended a work meeting at Harvard University. Among the state policymakers, researchers, and subject-matter experts sat a young child. His father, a state legislator, had brought him, and the two-year-old definitely didn't want to be there.

Most attendees mumbled under their breath in quiet disapproval as the child cycled mostly between exploring and crying. After several hours, the child approached my colleague, a nationally recognized policy expert and self-proclaimed proud grandfather. The little boy stretched out his arms and waited to be picked up. Without hesitation, my colleague scooped up the child, and—within minutes—he had gently rocked the little boy to sleep, all without missing a moment of the discussion at hand.

The moment reminded me of the many times I'd watched young children at church do anything to get their fathers' attention—tug on a pant leg, squirm in their chair—anything. They longed for their fathers to pick them up and hold them close. The kids showed no concern for others' thoughts toward them. They didn't hesitate or worry about being disciplined. Their primary goal was to receive love and care from their father.

Your Heavenly Father wants you to come to him with the same reckless abandonment. Do you find yourself struggling with the consequences of sin? Wrestling with doubt and fear? Desperate to change your circumstances? Weary from life's demands? Whatever it is, and wherever you find yourself spiritually, he invites—actually, he eagerly *desires*—for you to come to him. In his arms, you will find peace that passes all understanding, comfort that soothes your soul's deepest wounds, and rest that renews the weariest spirit.

Some may look down their noses at your surrender to Jesus in this way. They might even call your faith and dependence on God a "crutch." But don't allow these voices to discourage you. Jesus operates in another kind of kingdom—one where true strength is often found in our vulnerability before him.

In 2 Corinthians 12:9, the Lord tells Paul, "My grace is sufficient for you, for my power is made perfect in weakness." Our willingness to come to God with childlike dependence doesn't signify failure. Rather, it shows our acknowledgment that true power is found in his loving embrace, not in our self-sufficiency.

For those willing to throw off the things that keep us from falling into our Father's arms, we will find rest and security that extend into eternity. This rest doesn't result in an absence of struggle, but it does provide a deep-seated peace within the storm, since it allows us to know we are held. Think of Jesus sleeping in the boat during the tempest (Mark 4:38). His peace wasn't dependent on the absence of chaos, but on his unwavering trust in his Father. This same posture gives us the chance to feel his heartbeat, even if chaos surrounds us.

Perhaps your experience with your earthly father has been difficult or even harmful. If that is the case, I'm so sorry. Whatever pain or sorrow might be wrapped up in your relationship with your father, remember that you can bring it to your Heavenly Father, who is not a reflection of your earthly father, but rather the model of a perfect, sinless, and loving father. He knows every ache and crack in your heart, and he promises to meet you where you are now and not only once you've "gotten your act together." As James 4:8 encourages us, "Draw near to God, and he will draw near to you." Let that be an encouragement to you as you bring your raw and honest grief or weakness to God today.

LORD, *this has been a long season for me. At times, I've found it challenging to come to you, because by the world's standards I feel like I should be able to handle things on my own. Thank you, Lord, that I can't—and don't have to—do this by myself. Help me become like a child who is dependent on their Father for everything. Where my earthly father has disappointed and hurt me in the past, help me give those things to you, remembering that you alone are perfect. Remind me that with you all things are possible. You can give me all I need. Lord, I need your help to draw near to you. Thank you that in you I can find rest.*

IN JESUS'S NAME, *Amen.*

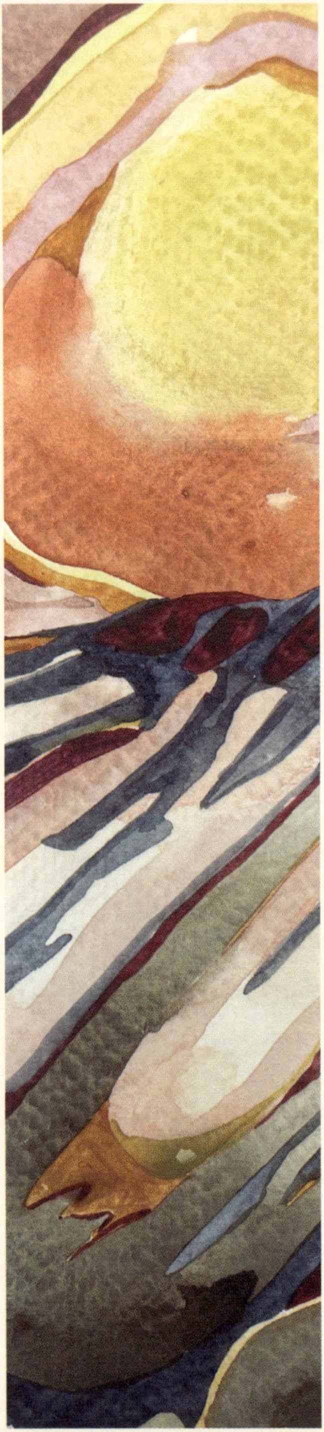

Share Your Story

PROMPT: Since you always have your Heavenly Father's unending and undivided attention, take some time to share with him what keeps you from resting in his arms. Ask him to help you release your grip on those things, so that you can freely rest in his presence.

ACTION STEP: From your perspective, what is the difference between simply accepting a weakness and embracing it? Choose one or two personal weaknesses and think through the steps you can take to move from simply accepting these weaknesses to embracing them. Act on the first step.

FOR LOVED ONES AND CAREGIVERS: How has the Lord used your time with your loved one to help you identify, accept, and embrace your own weaknesses? In what areas do you see opportunities for growth?

FOR PASTORS AND CHURCH LEADERS: Being in a safe environment, where people can be honest and vulnerable without fear of ridicule is important in learning how to embrace weakness and rest in God's arms. What strategies can you implement to foster such an environment for your congregation?

DAY 8

God Makes No Mistakes

YOU ARE HIS MASTERPIECE

For you formed my inward parts; you knitted me together in my mother's womb. I praise you, for I am fearfully and wonderfully made. . . . My frame was not hidden from you, when I was being made in secret, intricately woven in the depths of the earth. Your eyes saw my unformed substance; in your book were written, every one of them, the days that were formed for me, when as yet there was none of them.

Psalm 139:13–16

IN MY MIND'S EYE, I can see the rhythmic motion of my auntie's knitting needles in her hands. She would push the needle through the loop, wrap the yarn around the back side, then push the loop off one needle and onto the other. She would spend hours deeply engaged in conversation while her hands created an intricately patterned sweater or blanket, all seemingly without counting rows or stitches.

My older sister, Lila, and I longed to follow in her knitting footsteps as young teens. Despite multiple attempts, we eventually resigned ourselves to the truth that we lacked the required patience and attention to detail. The closest I came to knitting successfully was when I created a simple scarf, and even then, it lacked a discernible pattern, with some rows containing extra stitches and others missing them.

The Evolution of Disability Language and Identity

Scripture repeatedly reminds us of the weight our words carry. Our speech can bring healing or destruction, influencing our hearts, thoughts, and actions. God cares deeply about our speech and its delivery (Proverbs 15:1, Matthew 12:36). And no area of life is exempt—including the way we talk about disability.

As believers, reconciling Scripture's unchanging nature with the fluidity of language can be challenging. The criteria for what is acceptable seem to regularly shift. Historical events and scientific advancements have also transformed our understanding of disability, like so many aspects of our world.

Consider the label "handicapped." Although its origins trace back to a 1600s English game, "hand-in-cap," it later became associated with begging. Today, many consider it offensive, opposing its use on public signs. This reveals a common pattern. Words like "idiot" and "lunatic" began neutrally but later developed negative connotations.

Then there is "invalid" (frail, sick, injured). While distinct from "invalid" (null or void), the identical spelling stirs contention and feelings of invalidation. Similarly, some see "special needs" as a euphemism. They argue its use suggests discomfort with the word "disabled."

Some in the disability community have pushed back, transforming once pejorative terms into expressions of pride and solidarity. Terms like "cripple" (950 AD to the mid-twentieth century), "spaz," and "mad"—are now part of the community's shared identity.

Meaningful strides in language are good and necessary, but they don't resolve deeper discomfort or prejudice. That heart change requires the Holy Spirit's transformative work. Let's lean on him for the courage to use language that is honest rather than easy. Honoring the dignity and worth of every person, as God's image bearers, means speaking the truth with love.

Thankfully, we see a vastly different picture of knitting in Psalm 139:13, as the psalmist declared, "You formed my inward parts; you knitted me together in my mother's womb." The Hebrew word used for "inward parts"—*kilyah*—may refer to internal organs and one's inner self, or the heart. In the earlier verses of Psalm 139, the psalmist acknowledged that God knew his thoughts even before he spoke. He understood that God was aware of his every move—from his getting up in the morning to lying down at night. Even if he tried to go to the earth's farthest edges—either to the sea's deepest parts or to the morning's edge, God's Spirit—his presence—would always be there.

God's intimate awareness came not from his observations at a distance, but his interest and involvement even before the beginning of creation and from the psalmist's first moments of life. Consider this with me: God's presence fills creation from the depths of the waters to the outside edge of the sunrise. His love, care, and mindfulness reach to the farthest corners of the world. But here is an equally amazing truth: His love and concern for details extend to the deepest parts of *you*. If you doubt or question God's care in this way, consider these details:

- **FROM THE MOMENT OF FERTILIZATION,** a human embryo's genome consists of all the genetic information necessary for full development.
- **WHEN THE DNA** (deoxyribonucleic acid) from one human cell is stretched out, the resulting six-foot strand consists of a six billion letter code.
- **A HUMAN BODY'S DNA** is equal to twice the solar system's diameter.[23]
- **ACCORDING TO SCIENTISTS,** sufficient genetic variation exists such that no two humans will ever be genetically identical.[24]

Even without the scientific advancements of genetics and X-rays, the psalmist clearly saw God's creative power and purposeful design in the human body. It's no wonder he said, "I praise you, for I am fearfully and wonderfully made" (Psalm 139:14). The word "fearfully" refers to "awe" and can also mean "fearfully set apart" (for God's purposes).

The psalmist knew and believed in God's awareness of every detail of his life. He realized that God's plans for him preceded God's creation of him from the dust of the earth (Genesis 3:19). These truths were mind-blowing: "Such knowledge is too wonderful for me; it is high; I cannot attain it" (verse 6).

As a young believer, I recall thinking, *If God is so interested in me and concerned about the details of my life, why do I have a disability?* I continually wrestled with the lie that God did not care, or that he was absent in the earliest days and months of my life.

Then one day, God changed my heart. My thinking shifted from *Where was he?* to *God, because you care, I trust my disability isn't an accident. Give me a glimpse of the unique plans and purposes you have for me. Help me trust you and your ways. Use me in whatever way you want.*

If you question how or why God could or would allow your current pain and struggling, I invite you to consider your current situation from this perspective: God has knit each cell in your body. Your body and mind are not predetermined, standard parts simply put together in a unique way. You are a one-of-a-kind masterpiece, created by and for God. If God is so intentional, surely he has a purpose and a plan for your life.

LORD, *thank you that you have cared for me since before time began. You do not simply observe from afar. I can take comfort in knowing you pay attention to details. You have been intimately aware and involved in the making of every cell in my body. Not one nucleotide of my DNA has been misplaced. You created me and set me apart for your purposes. Although the world may label me based on my illness or disability, remind me that you do not label me. You see me as wholly unique and created for a purpose. Thank you.*

IN JESUS'S NAME, *Amen.*

Share Your Story

PROMPT: How do you feel about the label "disabled"? What has informed your perspective?

ACTION STEP: Create a "Fearfully and Wonderfully Made" journal, either on paper or on your phone. If writing is difficult, it's okay to simply think through this exercise. Start by writing the phrase "I am fearfully and wonderfully made" at the top of a page. Underneath, list at least five qualities or experiences that make you unique. This can include talents, interests, or moments of resilience. Be sure to include both challenges and triumphs.

Use drawings, colors, or collages to visually represent your journey. At the end of your journaling session, write an affirmation statement that reflects your inherent worth and identity beyond the label of "disability." For example, "I am a child of God. I am saved by grace."

FOR LOVED ONES AND CAREGIVERS: What perceptions of disability have informed how you treat or interact with your loved one or client with a disability? In what ways do these perceptions need to be challenged and how might doing so equip you to better support your loved one?

FOR PASTORS AND CHURCH LEADERS: If you have disabled people in your congregation, arrange a time to talk with at least one or two of them. If not, contact a local disability organization and arrange a conversation with at least one or two people with disabilities to get their perspectives on

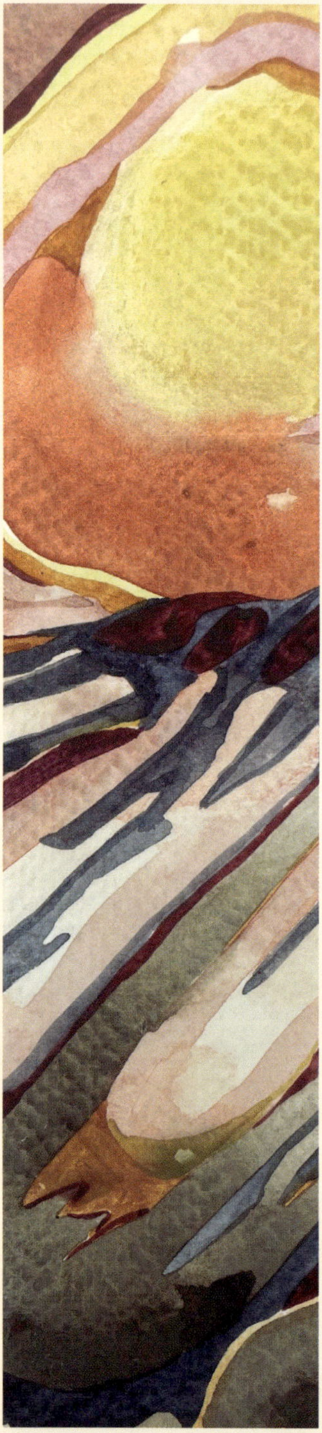

faith and disability. If you cannot identify one or two people, speak to someone else in the organization. How might learning from those with disabilities help inform innovative programs and/or help you better support your congregation?

DAY 9

Strengthen Your Inner Being

ASKING FOR HOLY SPIRIT POWER

For this reason I bow my knees before the Father, from whom every family in heaven and on earth is named, that according to the riches of his glory he may grant you to be strengthened with power through his Spirit in your inner being, so that Christ may dwell in your hearts through faith—that you, being rooted and grounded in love, may have strength to comprehend with all the saints what is the breadth and length and height and depth, and to know the love of Christ that surpasses knowledge, that you may be filled with all the fullness of God.

Ephesians 3:14–19

I KEPT REMINDING MYSELF that I was at the gym for Asher, the youngest of my three stepsons. He was on a one-week home visit from residential treatment. Program protocol required that either Mathew or I accompany Asher on all public outings. By joining Asher at the gym, I hoped to demonstrate an interest in body building, an activity that served as a lifeline for him.

Our silence as he pushed my manual wheelchair through the gym confirmed our mutual feelings of awkwardness. My presence jeopardized his fragile, mature, cool, and independent fifteen-year-old image. And, as a clearly nonathletic, disabled person, I wrestled with the voices in my head, convinced all watching eyes questioned my purpose in being there.

I carefully watched people of all sizes and shapes flaunt their strength in several ways: lifting barbells, running on treadmills, and balancing on exercise balls. I tried not to stare, but the combination of curiosity and self-consciousness took over. A longing for such clearly defined muscles and ease of movement momentarily overpowered contentment in my heart.

Perhaps you have experienced these feeling, too. Maybe illness, injury, or a lifelong disability has changed your physical abilities, affecting your strength and/or muscle tone. Maybe you have thought, *If I only had the physical strength to do this on my own, everything would be better, and I could more effectively glorify God*. Friend, that's a completely understandable and admirable thought, but in today's passage, we see that Paul wanted something far greater than increased physical strength or ability for the church in Ephesus.

The early church faced its own discouragements and challenges, one being that they had to navigate differences related to dietary practices and laws. But Paul's prayer in his letter to the Ephesians centered not on a superficial, worldly strength. Interestingly, he did not pray for the early believers to win arguments related to these dietary practices or laws. His prayerful request focused on the unique, immeasurable inner power given only by the Holy Spirit, the third person of the Trinity (God in three persons—God the Father, God the Son [Jesus], and God the Spirit).

He prayed longingly for a deep, abiding faith and an understanding of God's infinite love and power working within them.

As he kneeled before the Father, Paul acknowledged God's limitless resources—the riches of his glory. Other Scriptures explain that this "glory" referred not to material wealth but rather to the very essence of his being: his Spirit. He freely and generously gave—and still gives—the

Holy Spirit to strengthen our hearts and souls, and to help us grow as Jesus's followers.

When you accept Jesus's sacrifice for your sins, you receive the Holy Spirit as a "deposit" (2 Corinthians 1:22, NIV). With your acceptance, you are brought into a spiritual family, where Christ is the head. Christ himself dwells in your heart through faith—not through your physical strength, skill, or ability. The Holy Spirit's presence within every true believer demonstrates God's unwavering love and his commitment—a tangible promise—of your adoption into his family. It is the guarantee of Heavenly inheritance that awaits you.

This "down payment" serves as evidence that you are his, and that God's power is at work within you. Through the strength and grace of the Spirit, you can face any challenge that comes against you, because he empowers you.

In pain, trials, and weakness, the Holy Spirit comes alongside you, offering a peace that defies reason and understanding. He intercedes for you with wordless groans when you—in your weakness—don't know what to pray for (Romans 8:26). He gives you an inner strength that empowers you to follow and serve God in ways you otherwise could not do on your own.

The Holy Spirit also teaches you, reminding you what Jesus taught and what God's Word says. He gives you wisdom to understand God's Word. As Jesus explained in John 14:26 (NIV), "the Advocate, the Holy Spirit, whom the Father will send in my name, will teach you all things and will remind you of everything I have said to you."

This inner strengthening by the Holy Spirit should provide us with courage and hope that, despite any declining physical health or increasing adversities, his power within us will never diminish. Scripture also reminds us that even as our physical bodies decline, the Holy Spirit daily renews our inner being (2 Corinthians 4:16–18). In other words, he is daily making us—you—stronger. This strength anchors us in Christ's love and enables us to understand—in a manner that extends beyond mere intellectual knowledge—the unfathomable dimensions of his love.

Author Andrew Murray[25] describes the Holy Spirit's work and presence in believers this way:

> **The highest glory of the creature is in being only a vessel, to . . . show forth the glory of God. It can do this only as it is willing to be nothing in itself, that God may be all. . . . The lower, the emptier a man lies before God, the speedier and the fuller will be the inflow of the divine glory.**

Friend, be encouraged today that your true strength is not defined by outward appearance or physical ability but by the Holy Spirit's daily renewal of your inner being. Consider this truth: the third person of the Trinity—God himself—is not only your companion and comforter in the deep valleys of life, but he is also your strength and courage. If you question whether God's love is real, ask the Holy Spirit to help you see the depths of God's love for you. The Holy Spirit will do this and more. He will give you the strength to cling to Jesus.

LORD, *thank you that you are Emmanuel, God with us. Just as Paul prayed for the church at Ephesus, I ask you to strengthen me in my inner being. In your amazing grace and power, Jesus, remind me who I am in you. My trials and difficulties have weakened me physically and emotionally, and I often feel empty and lost. Bring to my mind and heart truths that have encouraged me in the past. At the same time, move in my heart in a new way. I yield myself to you, Lord. Fill me with your Holy Spirit. I ask that you do this not simply for my benefit, but for the good of your church and the building up of your body. Give me courage to continue on this challenging path, and please help me to glorify you in my weakness.*

IN JESUS'S NAME, *Amen.*

Share Your Story

PROMPT: In what areas of your life have you allowed outward ability to define your strength, either knowingly or inadvertently? Explain your answer. Describe the possible reason(s) for this and the impact that it has had on how you view yourself and your disability.

ACTION STEP: Reflect on the external circumstances that make you feel weak. What inner resources can help you navigate these situations (i.e., faith, the Holy Spirit, perseverance, and/or resilience)? Please explain your answer. What strategies have you used in the past to build inner strength?

FOR LOVED ONES AND CAREGIVERS: How do you define strength in yourself compared with those you care for with disabilities? Is there a difference? Why or why not?

FOR PASTORS AND CHURCH LEADERS: How do the traditional definitions of strength inform the church's teachings? How can you encourage recognition of divine inner strength? How can you equip your congregation to build inner strength?

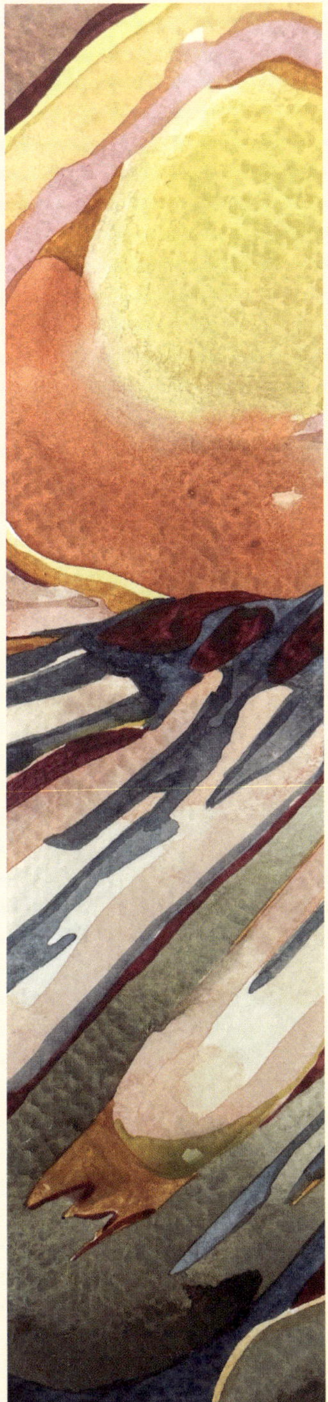

DAY 10

Staying on the Path

GOD'S STRENGTH IN YOUR LIMITATIONS

But he said to me, "My grace is sufficient for you,
for [M]y power is made perfect in weakness."
Therefore I will boast all the more gladly of my weaknesses,
so that the power of Christ may rest upon me.
For the sake of Christ, then, I am content with weaknesses,
insults, hardships, persecutions, and calamities.
For when I am weak, then I am strong.

2 Corinthians 12:9–10

LIVING WITH A DISABILITY sometimes leaves me weary and discouraged—tearfully begging and pleading God for healing. I know I'm not alone. Being in a fallen world means each of us is continuously either entering, enduring, or coming out of a trial-filled season. And while there's nothing wrong with asking for healing and deliverance in these seasons, sometimes our Heavenly Father responds differently than we anticipate.

Consider the apostle Paul's experience detailed in 2 Corinthians 12:9–10. Bible commentators explain that some members of the church in Corinth questioned Paul's legitimacy as an apostle, given that he endured "weaknesses, insults, hardships, persecutions, and calamities" (verse 10). But Paul said that these experiences provided opportunities to comfort others, to demonstrate God's power, and to testify to the sufficiency of God's grace.

Paul recounted pleading three times for the Lord to remove his "thorn . . . in the flesh." Although Scripture doesn't provide details about the affliction, we can assume it significantly affected Paul. Nowhere in the Bible do we read about God removing this thorn, yet he compassionately reassured Paul that divine grace was enough to strengthen and sustain him, despite his weaknesses. He said, "My grace is sufficient for you, for [m]y power is made perfect in weakness."

Bible dictionaries explain that this grace in the context of our relationship with God refers to his unmerited favor. So when he declared, "My grace is sufficient . . ." the implication is that God's grace is not simply adequate but rather everything we need. And it demonstrates the fullness and completeness of God's power to a watching world.

Effectively, God said to Paul (and to us): "Don't rely on human strength or effort to earn my love or demonstrate your worthiness or dedication. My love is a gift." As humans, we can extend grace to one another, but the same type of exchange—or any type of exchange, for that matter—is impossible with God. Nothing can match his grace, and he needs nothing from us. Given our weakness and deficiency, we must rely wholly on God's favor, which we can never earn.

In light of this truth, faith is the only fitting response. Hebrews 11:1 tells us that "[f]aith is the assurance of things hoped for, the conviction of things not seen." Assurance refers to a certainty—a confidence and trust. The Greek word used for "conviction" is ἔλεγχος (pronounced *elenchos*), which means prove or proof (or evidence). As we respond in faith—placing our confidence solely in this grace—our lives and actions are able to reflect the certainty of God's promises. They *prove* (or provide evidence for) the things not seen—the things of God. This same confident trust serves as an anchor for our souls, even when the outcome is invisible.

You may be tempted to believe that the "weaknesses, insults, hardships" you face render you ineffective, or (even worse) useless to God. But that is a lie from the enemy. Nothing could be further from the truth. God has blessed you and me with unique gifts and strengths, and there will always be ways we can share those to help others.

Furthermore, embracing our weaknesses and limitations and resting completely on God's grace displays his power and majesty like nothing else. I've seen this hold true in my life.

As explained in the introduction, I have CP, a central nervous system condition that affects the brain's messages to muscles. It affects my entire body, and my right side is worse than my left. Given my disability, I rely on others for assistance with my activities of daily living (ADLs).

But my inability to fully care for myself has been a window of opportunity God has used to display his power, faithfulness, and kindness—and the riches of his grace—in ways I never would've expected when he saved me at age eighteen. Ask him how he wants to use your life to demonstrate his love and grace.

LORD, *thank you that when I am weak and weary, you are strong. Help me remember that my challenges serve as opportunities for you to demonstrate the sufficiency of your grace to save and sanctify me. I need your encouragement today. Use me to testify to others. Remind me that I can't earn your unmerited favor. It is a gift. May I remember that the best response to this amazing gift is a life of faith that affirms the certainty of your promises and proves the hidden things of God.*

IN JESUS'S NAME, *Amen.*

Share Your Story

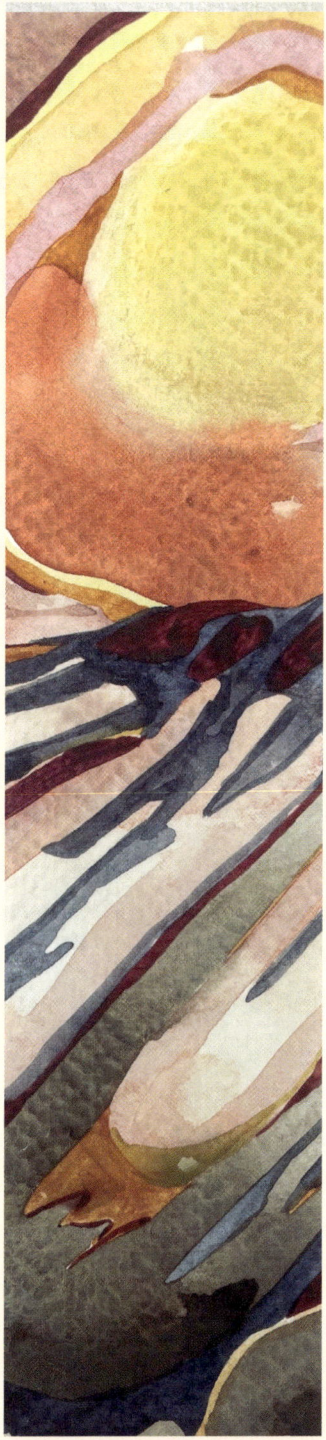

PROMPT: Consider answers to prayer that have been different than you expected. How have these instances impacted the way you pray? In what ways have the unexpected answers been blessings in disguise? How might these types of answers to prayer inform your response the next time you receive an unexpected answer?

ACTION STEP: Invite the Holy Spirit to reveal at least one area in your life through which God might desire to demonstrate his power, despite your personal feelings of weakness. Take time to pray about the area identified, and journal about any changes you see in the next few weeks and/or months.

FOR LOVED ONES AND CAREGIVERS: In what areas do you feel the weakest when it comes to supporting or caring for your loved one or client? Take some time to read, meditate, and reflect on 2 Corinthians 12:9–10. How do these verses change your thinking, and what practical implications might this have for you?

FOR PASTORS AND CHURCH LEADERS: In what ways do your own misconceptions about strength and weakness keep you from recognizing God's glory in those you may consider the most vulnerable members of your congregation (e.g., those with disabilities, chronic illnesses, or mental health conditions)?

Navigating Transformative Ground

Building Strength and Vision

DAY 11

Being Courageous

REFLECTING DIVINE COMPANIONSHIP

Have I not commanded you? Be strong and courageous.
Do not be frightened, and do not be dismayed,
for the LORD your God is with you wherever you go.

Joshua 1:9

"I WOULD NEVER marry or date someone with a disability."

The statement, delivered with no eye contact and a heaping dose of awkwardness, landed on the table between me and my latest date. The most discouraging part: I'd heard similar sentiments in the past from other men. And, as always, I could only sit there, too stunned to say anything. While I had experienced God's blessings in so many areas of life, romantic relationships remained my Achilles' heel. With the few men that had expressed interest, I always ended the relationships before they began, which usually reflected my lack of self-confidence more than anything else.

In 2015, my participation in the Bold Beauty Project Photo Exhibit, created to highlight the beauty of women with disabilities, shattered my long-held false beliefs and insecurities about myself. Participating in the event represented far more to me than a simple nod to beauty or a chance to advocate for women with disabilities. God used the process to rebuild my confidence in who and how he had made me.

Since participation in the event meant sharing part of my story on the event website, I seized the opportunity to say, "Some people will let their own perceptions and stereotypes keep them from experiencing the full beauty of life that may cross their life path. . . . It's counterproductive to spend time worrying about what others think of me. I have come to believe and understand every part of me is wonderfully made."[26]

My experience of stepping into courage during that event reminds me of Esther's story in the Bible. Although the Lord is not explicitly mentioned in the Old Testament book of Esther, Bible scholars agree that the Lord's fingerprints are evident throughout the book. You may recall the story begins with the king of Persia, Xerxes, holding a beauty contest following Queen Vashti's refusal to comply with his request to flaunt herself in front of party guests. Esther's cousin, Mordecai suggested she participate in the contest. She captured the king's attention and was crowned queen. Later, Mordecai reminded Esther of her divinely appointed position: Her willingness to plead with the king could potentially protect Mordecai and save the Jewish people. In the end, Esther courageously approached the king without a formal invitation, a practice strictly forbidden. Her bravery saved her uncle and the Jewish people.

You may not be called to participate in a beauty contest or rescue an entire people group. But, don't be too quick to dismiss an opportunity to demonstrate courage and trust in God. Maybe God is calling you to be brave in a relationship. Or perhaps you feel prompted to speak up about your experiences, lack of accessibility, care, work, accommodations, or ableism in the church. Or perhaps it's something else. You may be thinking, *That's a small thing. Should I really say something?* Or, *I'm afraid the situation is too complicated and beyond my ability to address. Will anything I say or do really have influence?*

Previous negative experiences may make you reluctant to say or do something, especially if you don't want to "rock the boat." Maybe you're wondering if you have enough strength and bravery to speak up or act on what the Holy Spirit may bring to your attention. But if you look only to your strength or skill to build or exercise courage, you'll come up short every time, regardless of how long you've followed Jesus.

As I learned in my dating experiences and through the Bold Beauty Project: It's not the size of our courageous action that matters, but rather the source of our courage. And when Jesus is the source of our courage, we can move forward in spite of fear.

Jesus himself experienced moments of needing to be courageous. In the Garden of Gethsemane, his soul was so deeply troubled by the thought of going to the cross that he sweat drops of blood. And yet, he neither fought back nor ran away. Instead, "for the joy that was set before him," he "endured the cross, despising the shame, and is seated at the right hand of the throne of God" (Hebrews 12:2).

Whatever you're facing, Jesus is the one from whom and in whom you can draw courage. So I encourage you to spend time with him. Get to know him as your source of courage. Study his words and his life. And, as Zechariah 4:10 wonderfully communicates, don't be afraid to start small. God honors and loves even the smallest acts of courage.

Of course, practicing courage won't fix everything. You may still have to deal with bad dates or hurtful comments. But whenever you feel stretched beyond your comfort zone, cling tightly to the One who exemplifies true courage—and who never leaves your side. If you're feeling scared or anxious about how others will respond to your acts of courage, fix your eyes on Jesus. Do not give others the power to speak into or influence your life with demeaning words. Instead, trust the Lord to fill you with peace and his assurance. You are a child of God, and he alone has the final word in your life.

If you're a believer, remember that you come from a long line of courageous saints who believed God and followed him in spite of significant opposition and even death. Read Hebrews 11 and recall the stories of Abraham, Noah, Sarah, and Rahab. They all trusted God and took brave steps forward despite very challenging circumstances. Since biblical times, millions more have anchored their courage in Jesus, the Cornerstone.

So, fix your gaze on him, and you will be able to experience a courage that can weather life's harshest storms. Most importantly, remember that God may have created you "for such time as this" (Esther 4:14).

LORD, *you are the source and the reason for my courage. Help me to know you better, so I may grow in courage. Comfort my heart with this truth today and in the days ahead. Remind me that you have uniquely designed a path for me. Whether I can see what's up ahead or whether I'm facing the unknown, I can cling to this certainty: You promise to never leave me or forsake me. I can move forward even if I fear, because my strength comes from you. You will be with me wherever I go.*

IN JESUS'S NAME, *Amen.*

Share Your Story

PROMPT: In what areas do you feel the Lord encouraging you to be strong and courageous? What are your most significant barriers (e.g., time, money, transportation, other supports, etc.)? What are your biggest psychological, emotional, or spiritual hurdles (e.g., fear, lack of self-confidence, etc.)?

ACTION STEP: Identify a few goals you would like to accomplish. Consider each goal's investment level (i.e., personal time and/or money). Break larger or more complex goals into smaller, more manageable goals or steps. Finally, review the goals and their corresponding investment levels. Choose a short-term goal requiring low-level investment to work on over the next two weeks. Continue working your way down your goal list, moving from the easiest to more difficult.

FOR LOVED ONES AND CAREGIVERS: In what ways have others' expectations of your strength affected your ability to thoroughly process difficulties you've faced? What difficulties have you not yet worked through? Take some time to journal about them, and identify ways you can create time and space to work through some of them.

FOR PASTORS AND CHURCH LEADERS: What are some ways you can demonstrate that courage can involve being vulnerable and present with people who are suffering, rather than feeling the pressure to "fix" or "heal" them? From your perspective, what does it mean to "be with" someone in their pain, even when you don't have all the answers?

DAY 12

Pursuing Justice

IDENTIFYING INEQUITIES

He has told you, O man, what is good;
and what does the LORD require of you but to do justice,
and to love kindness, and to walk humbly with your God?

Micah 6:8

LIGHTNING STRUCK the electrical box that controlled the locking mechanism of my condo building's main door, and somehow the condo board held me responsible for the $1,200 repair. Their logic baffled me.

I reached out to my condominium board, reminding them that any resident could purchase the special remote I used to bypass the key fob function. Fellow residents had multiple alternatives for accessing the building, including a standard key and a back entrance, which did not meet accessibility standards. I only had one way into the building and—by extension—my condominium unit. The lightning strike had rendered me dependent on someone else opening the building's front door simply so I could enter my living space.

I tried for weeks to navigate the situation with the condominium board without help from an outside entity, but we had reached an impasse. I called the county's Human Rights Commission, which investigated discrimination complaints and incidents of hate/violence. Within several days, an investigator came to gather details about the situation, which included taking pictures. Several weeks later, the commission notified me that the condominium board held responsibility for the repair. The board's attempt to have me pay for the repair was determined by the commission to be discriminatory.

If you have a disability or have spent time with a disabled person, you have likely witnessed firsthand some of the inequities faced by people with disabilities. These inequities may occur in connection with various systems or on an individual level. Systemic challenges include barriers to accessible, reliable transportation; difficulty accessing

Disability and the Church

The American church and the disability community share a complex relationship. Tension began with the introduction of the Americans with Disabilities Act (ADA) in Congress in 1989. Since then, "religious groups, particularly the American church, have aggressively resisted participation," arguing that mandating participation would constitute "government interference."

Legal counsel representing many organizations in the Christian community explained that no evidence existed to demonstrate "the necessity" of applying the ADA to "churches, religious schools, and other ministries." In the end, "Christians stood nearly alone against access for disabled people" becoming an equal part of religious groups. Many in the disability community interpreted this to mean they "did not belong in mainstream U.S. Christianity."[27]

Since that time, a growing number of churches have established disability ministries. In addition, denominations and parachurch ministries have provided resources and assistance to facilitate the inclusion of the disabled and their families.

appropriate healthcare; or a lack of disability-inclusive, work-based learning opportunities. On an individual level, inequities may show up in the form of discrimination, stigma, and pity. These injustices often exist as a result of systemic or individual problems, genuine oversight, or a focused attempt to disadvantage or exclude disabled people.

Jesus's teachings and example stand in stark contrast to these types of inequities. As a result, you may wrestle with how to appropriately respond to inequities in light of personal beliefs and biblical truths. For example, you may hold to the Christian view that everyone is equal at the foot of the cross: We all sin and fall short, but God forgives and saves all who place their trust in Christ. And, regardless of your background, socioeconomic status, or previous sin, you know you are a child of God who deserves to be treated with dignity and respect.

So how should we respond when the world often fails to treat us this way?

Micah 6:8, originally addressed to the leaders of the Southern Kingdom of Judah, provides a broad framework for identifying inequalities and pursuing justice.

- **ACT JUSTLY:** Jesus took on our sins and died in our place, and through this act, justice was served. As his children, we are now in him and have access to everything he gives us. On a practical level, because we have received this undeserved grace and mercy, we should show the same grace to vulnerable populations. This goes beyond simply ensuring that everyone, including those with disabilities, has access to the same opportunities. Acting justly also means providing people with everything they need to perform at their best, considering their unique needs.

  Just as the Lord deals with each of his children individually, it is vital to recognize the unique circumstances and needs that individuals and groups face. As followers of Jesus, we don't need to fear that one person or group is receiving favorable treatment. Resting in God's sovereignty and generosity allows us to care for and extend grace to the most vulnerable among us. We should pursue circumstances where there is a legitimate issue and make every effort to resolve issues prior to taking formal legal action.

If you are interested in advancing justice for people with disabilities, consider your own skills and interests. For example, if you have experience in the healthcare field, consider volunteering at a local health clinic or nonprofit organization that advances healthcare options for the underserved. Another option might be visiting local nursing homes or assisted living facilities to spend time with residents. Offer a person with a disability a ride to church, or ask your church leaders if anyone needs help with transportation, light housekeeping, or grocery shopping. Search online for both virtual and in-person volunteer opportunities. If you have limited resources, consider simply getting to know a neighbor.

LOVE KINDNESS: Genuine kindness goes a long way in sharing the love of Christ to people who may not attend church. As you figure out unique ways to love others, remember how the Lord saved you and recall his kindness to you. Look for practical, everyday opportunities to meet the needs of disabled people and their families, and don't be afraid to ask how you can best serve them. Take time to get to know individuals and families and let them bless you in the ways they are able. This helps create a balance in the relationship and recognizes that everyone has gifts or talents they can share with the world around them.

WALK HUMBLY: Since your attitude and actions can significantly impact your witness, pursue justice in a manner that fosters dialogue. Don't assume you know what's best or right for someone based on your own experiences. Acknowledge your imperfections, including the truth that you, like each of us, have wronged others and God. Remind yourself that God's mercy and kindness resulted in your salvation, even when you didn't deserve it. Pursuing justice may be your calling, but be careful not to let anger and frustration consume you. It is never acceptable to harm others through our words or actions all in the name of justice. In the end, we can only do our best and leave the deep work of exacting justice to God. Sometimes, you may have to surrender an issue and simply rest in God's goodness and sovereignty.

LORD, *thank you that you love justice. Give me eyes to see the needs of people around me, and help me respond in a way that honors you. It can be so easy to carry a chip on my shoulder, but you call me to walk humbly and love kindness. Please show me what that looks like in different situations. I ask for your wisdom and grace as I face challenges, knowing that you have the final word. Help me to navigate difficult encounters in a way that honors you, Lord.*

IN JESUS'S NAME, *Amen.*

Share Your Story

PROMPT: Do you agree or disagree with the elements of justice described above (act justly, love kindness, walk humbly)? Why or why not? What would you add or change?

ACTION STEP: Is there an individual or systemic injustice that you are particularly passionate about? Study the positions of various disability organizations on that particular topic, and then think about ways you can use your expertise to advance policy for change on the issue.

FOR LOVED ONES AND CAREGIVERS: How might you carry the burden of advocacy on behalf of a loved one with a disability? How can you better empower that person to pursue justice for themselves? If that's not possible, how can you better involve them in your efforts on their behalf?

FOR PASTORS AND CHURCH LEADERS: In what ways, if any, do you encourage church members to pursue justice for people with disabilities or for underserved people groups in the community? What more could be done? How familiar are you with the needs of particular individuals or families in your congregation? If someone were to call you and ask how they can help someone in the church, what would you say to them?

DAY 13

Persevering on Rough Terrain

LEARNING RESILIENCY THROUGH ADVERSITY

Humble yourselves, therefore, under the mighty hand of God so that at the proper time he may exalt you, casting all your anxieties on him, because he cares for you. Be sober-minded; be watchful. Your adversary the devil prowls around like a roaring lion, seeking someone to devour. Resist him, firm in your faith, knowing that the same kinds of suffering are being experienced by your brotherhood throughout the world. And after you have suffered a little while, the God of all grace, who has called you to his eternal glory in Christ, will himself restore, confirm, strengthen, and establish you.

1 Peter 5:6–10

I TYPICALLY WAKE UP a few hours before my assistant arrives at seven a.m. I read my Bible, respond to emails, and do whatever work I can from my phone. But on one particular day, negative thoughts consumed me even before I opened my eyes. It was like Fear, Worry, Anxiety, Loneliness, and Tiredness had called an emergency meeting in my head and were demanding my full attention:

You are not going to make it.
What's the next big thing that's going to happen?
You know, bad things always happen in threes.
Who is going to get sick next?
No one wants to hear your negative news.
Your friends are tired of praying for you.

I lay in bed, trying to muster enough strength to face the day. I didn't want to get up, and I certainly didn't want to talk to anyone. I was tired. Tired of my life. Tired of needing help with my daily activities. Tired of the struggles. I wrestled against the urge to simply pull up the covers, tell my assistant to leave, and sleep my day away.

But then, I heard another voice in my head. Calmly, yet authoritatively, it seemed to say, *But you are still breathing, so God is not done with you yet.*

Can you relate with mornings or moments like these? Do the trials of life ever leave you struggling to get through the next minute, hour, or day with your disability? If you find yourself facing challenges or inner voices like these more often than not, hold on to this wisdom from 1 Peter 5:6–10, which gives guidance on how we can remain resilient amid trials:

- **HUMBLE YOURSELF UNDER THE LORD'S LOVING HAND AND CARE.** You may feel like you need to muster enough strength and motivation to face the rough moments of life. Scripture's guidance communicates a vastly different response in times like this. When you're feeling overwhelmed or alone, don't rely on your own wisdom to navigate life's hard seasons. You may be tempted to wrestle with God and beg him to shorten your time of trial. But know this: Your loving Father will not let you suffer one day longer than absolutely necessary, and he is using your time of trial to accomplish what he has planned for you.

- **TURN TO JESUS, TRUSTING THAT** your comforter, defender, king, brother, savior, and high priest cares for you. Nothing happens apart from his loving care. He understands your struggles, protects you, walks with you, and saves you. He intercedes on your behalf, even when you don't know what to pray.

LAY DOWN YOUR TENDENCY TO TRUST IN YOUR OWN STRENGTH. If you're feeling frustrated or impatient, you may be tempted to "take matters into your own hands," desperately grasping for any control while disregarding what might be practical or even healthy. Instead, challenge yourself to allow God to work in and through you in whatever trial you're facing. Imagine yourself giving Jesus your burdens. Place them at his feet and invite him to accomplish his purposes in your life. He has called you, and he himself will restore, confirm, strengthen, and establish you after the time of suffering is over.

PREPARE TO SUFFER FOR A LITTLE WHILE. Obviously, suffering is no fun, but keep in mind that God hates our pain even more than we do. But because we live in a fallen world, Jesus said this life would have trouble (John 16:33) regardless of age, socioeconomic status, race, ethnicity, family history, or abilities. These trials will look different for every person, but no one is without difficulty. So, much like a runner prepares for a marathon, you should prepare yourself for times of suffering. This may include storing God's word in your heart through Scripture memorization and regular quiet times with God. You can also feed your soul with encouraging books, podcasts, and other resources that give you a deeper understanding of God's character. Ask him to give you wisdom about what's ahead and to show you other ways you can prepare. Being prepared won't prevent the suffering, but it will equip you to face the road ahead with more grace and strength. And don't be discouraged if the "little while" goes longer than expected. God has promised he will always be with you, and after the hardships, Jesus will wipe away every tear (Rev 21:4).

UNDERSTAND THE PURPOSE OF TRIALS IN THE CHRISTIAN LIFE. Being in the middle of a tough season can narrow your vision by leaving little mental or emotional energy to focus on anything other than the here and now. But even in the worst circumstances, God can work all things together for the good of those who love him. Your suffering can be used to grow your faith, reveal his power, and serve his greater plan. Sometimes, your only choice in these times is to deliberately anchor yourself in God's promises for the future, as Jesus did (Hebrews 12:2). Much like the purification of gold, trials tend to reveal areas in your life where God wants to work. So as you fix your eyes on Jesus, allow him to make you more like himself. Notice insecurities, doubts, or areas where you experience anger or impatience when God allows a trial. He's not trying to trick you or watch you stumble. Rather, he may be refining you or drawing you closer to him. Difficulties can also bring together and strengthen the body of believers, so don't be afraid to share your burdens with others and to let others share theirs with you.

CAST YOUR ANXIETIES ON HIM. When negative thoughts threaten to overwhelm you, remember God cares for you (1 Peter 5:7). In his economy, our circumstances are not a reflection of his heart toward you. He is not far off. He is Immanuel, God with you. Even if you can't always sense him, he is deeply involved in your life and wants you to come to him with anything troubling you. Lay any fears, desires, and hopes at his feet.

RESIST THE ENEMY, AND KNOW YOU ARE NOT ALONE. Where God is at work, there will be spiritual warfare. Many moments of hardship or negative spirals may be a form of spiritual attack. After all, the enemy will not leave you alone willingly or easily. You must be on the lookout. One of the greatest lies the enemy uses to discourage and distract you is that your struggles are unique. "No one will understand," he whispers. "God doesn't care. He is denying you something good." But believers throughout the world struggle with similar lies. In the war for your soul, remember that Satan does not easily surrender. Meditate on God's promises. Also, keep in mind that the enemy must seek permission to touch you (Job 1:12). So, resist the enemy by keeping your eyes focused on Jesus and taking shelter in him.

Of course, learning to persevere through difficulties does not happen overnight. Remember: It is not a sin to struggle. Wrestling in trials helps strengthen your faith and build your endurance. This is not something you can accomplish by yourself. Holding tightly to Jesus is essential and builds hope in your heart. He is with you every step of the way and will keep you from falling. When you feel like you can't go on, remember that he is the Author and Perfector of your faith. He will finish the good work he began in you.

LORD, *thank you for enduring the cross on my behalf. Because of your sacrifice, I can persevere with hope, even when my faith is tested. As I face trials, please give me the strength and courage to continue following you. I'm so grateful for the companionship of the Holy Spirit. Please protect my mind and heart from doubt and fear. Remind me to put on the full armor of God. On my darkest days, remind me that you are with me for your praise and glory. Keep my focus on you, Lord. I trust that you will complete the good work you've started in my life. Give me eyes to see these challenges the way you see them: already defeated.*

IN JESUS'S NAME, *Amen.*

Share Your Story

PROMPT: Some may assume that resiliency improves as an individual endures more trials and hardships. In your experience, is this true or not? Please explain your answer. Have you become more or less resilient over time? Why do you think that is?

ACTION STEP: If you were to prepare to "suffer a little while," please describe some of the "tools" you would keep in your toolbox, in addition to your Bible? This could include specific Scripture verses that are meaningful to you, a particular song, or your favorite book. Please explain why these "tools" would be included in your toolbox. Have fun with this step!

FOR LOVED ONES AND CAREGIVERS: Of the strategies described in this devotion for remaining resilient amid trials, which one—in your opinion—is most helpful? Why? Would you add any other strategies? Please explain.

FOR PASTORS AND CHURCH LEADERS: On a scale of one to ten, with one being the lowest and ten being the highest, how would you rate the resiliency of your congregation as a whole? In what ways can the teachings and activities of your church cultivate and support resiliency for members who may be facing long-term challenges?

DAY 14

Discovering Beauty in Every Season

SEEING PURPOSE IN CHANGE

For I know the plans I have for you, declares the LORD, plans for welfare and not for evil, to give you a future and a hope.

Jeremiah 29:11

I NEVER ENVISIONED moving back in with my parents at the age of twenty-eight, but—as strange as it may sound—I was thankful and relieved to be with them. Time at my parents' home always brought peace and rest. It also often preceded significant changes in my life. Leaving my position at the publishing company certainly stung, but cautious optimism whispered to me that a future designed by the Lord was just around the corner.

During that unplanned season of change, I did all I knew to do. I prayed, stayed connected to my church family, and continued to pursue professional development opportunities. As I prayed for wisdom and direction about next steps, two ideas repeatedly resurfaced: a growing desire to help other disabled people achieve independence and the need to improve my skills to expand my career options. With these in mind, I spent some time researching career opportunities in different fields.

Eventually, I felt the Lord leading me to return to school. I applied to the University of Illinois Urbana-Champaign and was thrilled when I was accepted into their social work program. By the summer of 2000, I had completed my prerequisite courses at a university near my parents' home and entered graduate school.

As you might know from your own seasons of doubt, uncertainty, or despair, change often comes with mixed emotions. You might experience sadness for all you leave behind even as you feel joyful anticipation—or perhaps fear—for the surprises on the horizon. Maybe your life hasn't gone as you planned, but you've been able to see—in the beauty among the ashes—the kindness and faithfulness of God.

Given God's encouragement and instruction to the Israelites in Jeremiah, they likely felt some of these same mixed emotions. While your circumstances certainly differ significantly from the Israelites, principles from Jeremiah 29 can inform your response to seasons of change and growth:

PRAY: This may seem like a simple and obvious step to take, but don't underestimate its impact. Whether you're facing a difficult decision or a challenging season, ask God to direct your steps, and look for what he might want to do in and through you. You can also turn your prayers outward. Praying for your neighbors, your church, and the city allows you to take part in God's work in a particular location. The Bible also encourages us to pray for our leaders, which can include local leaders. Through prayer, you can help carry the burden of your friends and neighbors, build connections, and serve your community.

BUILD: Instead of waiting for life to return to its old "normal," consider that the Lord may be using change to guide you toward a "new normal," strengthening your flexibility and adaptability. Though staying in your "comfort zone" is tempting, you may be called to "build houses and live in them"—a metaphor for establishing a new life or routine shaped by the people and places God brings into your path.

PLANT: Settling and building relationships in a new place can feel overwhelming. But consider asking the Lord to help you "establish roots" wherever he wants you. In Acts 17:26–27, planting implies staying in one area for an entire growing season. You might look for work or a volunteer position as a means of gaining professional experience. You could also get involved in a local church, which can be a great place to strengthen your faith and meet new people.

INVEST: God may call you to do things that defy logic. For example, you might know that you won't be in an area or group for a long time, so you might choose not to invest practically or relationally. But God may call you to invest in that place or those people, which could potentially lead to more permanent ties. You never know when God may call you to establish new rhythms of life.

In any season of change, remember that God has specific plans for you. He may not call you to pursue change in each of these areas, but he does have a purpose in the change. Trust that his purposes are good for you, even if you can't see the end result yet.

LORD, *the pieces of my broken dreams surround me. I feel like I'm only able to focus on what I've lost. Help me lift my eyes to you. Encourage my heart and remind me that you are a promise-keeping God. Help me to pray, build, plant, and invest right where I am today. Make your words so alive in my heart that I'm not tempted to chase after empty promises or false teaching. Thank you, Lord, that in your timing, you will give me a vision for what's next. Help me pursue Your purposes amid change.*

IN JESUS'S NAME, *Amen.*

Share Your Story

PROMPT: As you think about a past season of change, describe the circumstances and feelings surrounding that season. What was the most difficult aspect of that season or the reason you found that aspect so difficult? What lessons did you learn?

ACTION STEP: When considering "Pray," "Build," "Plant," and "Invest," which element seems most relevant to where you are today? Please explain and share what activities you've been a part of during this time.

FOR LOVED ONES AND CAREGIVERS: Think about the ways others in your life have helped you in seasons of change. What did you find most helpful? How can that inform your support for your client or loved one in their season of change?

FOR PASTORS AND CHURCH LEADERS: How can the church create an environment that encourages openness and honesty in difficult seasons of change? Consider what is currently in place. What needs to be put in place to better serve the congregation in the future? Recall a time in ministry when shattered dreams resulted in new visions for you personally or for the church as a whole. What were some of your key lessons learned in that season? How can they be used to encourage those in your congregation who may be struggling in a difficult season?

DAY 15

Developing Survival Skills

PRAYING WITH PERSISTENCE

And he told them a parable to the effect that they ought always to pray and not lose heart. He said, "In a certain city there was a judge who neither feared God nor respected man. And there was a widow in that city who kept coming to him and saying, 'Give me justice against my adversary.' For a while he refused, but afterward he said to himself, 'Though I neither fear God nor respect man, yet because this widow keeps bothering me, I will give her justice, so that she will not beat me down by her continual coming.'"

Luke 18:1–5

"WHAT DO YOU DO if no one is around, and you need to open the door?" asked my friend Leah.

She was referring to our apartment building's back door: the only accessible entrance for the complex. She had opened the same door for me a few months earlier. At that time, we quickly bonded over the fact that we attended the same church and lived in the same apartment complex.

"I pray that someone walks by," I explained simply. She looked surprised for a moment. I could tell that wasn't the answer she expected.

"Oh yeah, that makes sense," she responded with a smile.

Some friends and family had expressed concerns about my living independently, working full-time, and being so far from family. Although I shared some of their reservations, I also held a deep belief that the Lord had led me to Washington, DC. This fact spurred me to pray with confidence, trusting that God would provide down to the smallest detail. All I needed to do was ask him. And ask I did for many things, including:

- **PICKING UP MY DROPPED KEYS** on my walk to the subway at six a.m., when I was in between service dogs and no one was in sight;
- **INTERVIEWING, HIRING,** and firing assistants;
- **GETTING BACK HOME** when accessible public transportation didn't show up, and I was nowhere near a train station;
- **TRAVELING TO AND FROM** Indiana independently, which included navigating the shuttle, then the airport and plane;
- **COMMANDING A NEW SERVICE DOG,** who tested my limits, especially when we were alone, and when I desperately needed him to do something for me.

Before I began following Jesus, I remember feeling confused by prayer. My earliest introduction to this important spiritual practice took place at my friend's house. As her family prayed for the meal, I simply bowed my head. Afterward, my friend's younger brother asked, "Mom, why didn't Nadia fold her hands?" I felt like I had committed the biggest faux pas.

As I began to explore faith on my own, I encountered different approaches to prayer from loud, boisterous requests to quiet, meditative prayers characterized by genuflection and the sign of the cross. Since then, I've learned that prayer is a very personal, spiritual practice with many different approaches.

In the simplest of terms, prayer gives you the opportunity to talk to God about anything at any time. No need for special clothing or an offering. He is not annoyed or frustrated by continual prayers. As a loving father, he wants to develop relationships with his children, and prayer is the way we engage in conversation with him.

Through Jesus's sacrifice, he removed the barrier between a holy God and sinful humanity. Prayer maintains this connection, allowing you to express your deepest fears, thanks, and desires, knowing God hears and understands your heart. Such intimate conversations strengthen your trust in God and remind you that you are his child.

Whether you've never prayed before or you're a seasoned prayer warrior, Jesus's guidance around prayer offers some parameters to consider:

- ASK ABOUT HIS AGENDA for you rather than simply telling him what you want (Matthew 6:10).
- PRAY WITH SINCERITY, not for show (Matthew 6:5). Your goal with prayer should not be to get attention or praise from others. Like anyone getting to know another person, God desires your full attention and honest conversation, which may at times mean going into your room, closing the door, and talking to God alone.
- USE SIMPLE AND HONEST WORDS (Matthew 6:7). There is no need to try to impress God with fancy words and big phrases. He already knows what you need. He simply wants to have an honest conversation with no pretense.
- HAVE FAITH, believing that God hears and answers prayers (Mark 11:24). If you question your faith when he doesn't answer your prayers as expected, consider this: If someone you love and trust doesn't always do what you want them to do, do you stop loving them? No, of course not. In the same way, God always hears your requests, and he always answers, even if that answer isn't what you expect.
- DON'T BE AFRAID OR HESITANT to keep knocking at the door. He will respond. Sometimes your prayers may be answered with a *no* or *not yet*. But that doesn't mean you should stop asking. He desires a genuine relationship rather than simply a transactional one. He wants to hear from you, but he also wants to share things with you.

When you pray, invite God to work in and through you and through your daily activities. As you spend time in his presence and focus on his character, the Holy Spirit will begin to transform your heart and mind. This process, called sanctification, will make you more patient, loving, and humble—reflecting the very nature of Jesus. In other words, prayer should be less about changing God's mind and more about God changing your heart.

THANK YOU, *Lord, that you've made a way to come to you directly. Thank you for caring enough about me and all the details of my life that you want to bend down and listen to me. Invite me into a continual conversation with you, Lord. Remind me that I'm not bothering you when I come to you with a worry, a hurt, or even a complaint. Teach me to cultivate a regular prayer rhythm with you. And help me be a prayer warrior for those around me.*

IN JESUS'S NAME, *Amen.*

Share Your Story

PROMPT: As you spend some time with God today, consider any areas of your life where you have been reluctant to talk to God. Identify the reasons behind your hesitancy.

ACTION STEP: Confess your struggle to bring up this area with him, and ask him to help you become more comfortable in sharing your whole heart. Take some time to listen to God's response to you, then write it in a journal or on your phone. That way, you can easily remind yourself what he shared with you.

FOR LOVED ONES AND CAREGIVERS: Sometimes as a caregiver, finding time for yourself can be challenging. Ask the Lord to help you make time for prayer, and then listen for his response. Have you ever considered praying with your loved one or client? If not, why not? Remember, you can always pray with them, even if they are not verbal or able to fully comprehend the prayer. Trust the Lord to work in their heart.

FOR PASTORS AND CHURCH LEADERS: Identify strategies to strengthen the prayer life of your entire congregation, including those with disabilities. Establish opportunities for your church family to pray for one another, if none currently exist. Make sure this opportunity is accessible to those with various disabilities. For those with cognitive disabilities, consider creating a visual guide or resource to assist them in prayer. Connect with individuals or their families to determine the most helpful type of resource.

Enjoying Hidden Oases

Embracing Uniqueness and Cultivating Joy

DAY 16

Speaking Up

ADVOCATING FOR CHANGE

Open your mouth, judge righteously,
defend the rights of the poor and needy.

Proverbs 31:9

MY OWN INTERNAL DIALOGUE had begun during our church members' meeting.

Should I say something? I don't want to come across as an angry person with a disability who finds every reason to complain about all accessibility failures. Yes, say something, because no one has brought up the topic. If church leaders are interested in drawing people in, having a push button at the front and bathroom doors sends an important message.

As I continued to deliberate with myself, I listened to a consulting firm share ideas about how to maximize existing space for our growing congregation. Our senior pastor then opened the floor for feedback.

I raised my hand.

"As we think about making changes to parts of the building and the parking lot," I started, my voice noticeably nervous, "I'm just curious if any consideration will be given to increasing access for people with disabilities?"

A silence fell across the room. From the looks on the faces of the consultant and one of the elders, I had clearly caught them off guard. The consultant then confirmed that accessibility would be a consideration.

"Okay, that's great, because I find both the bathroom and the main entrance doors difficult to navigate," I noted, wanting to point out some existing accessibility issues that could be fixed with the renovation.

Following the meeting, both the senior pastor and an elder approached me and asked for more details about my concerns with the front and bathroom doors. That evening they began planning the structural changes necessary to install push buttons for both doors.

Whether you are new to advocacy or have been an advocate for most of your life, finding your own voice is critical. Keep in mind that, in some respects, advocating for yourself and advocating for particular issues use different strategies. Advocating for yourself typically stems from individual experiences or interactions, particularly if you have been treated unfairly or disrespectfully. In these situations, it's helpful to know how existing laws or policies apply to your situation.

In contrast, advocating for general, larger system issues does not necessarily require personal experience. However, it is helpful. Given the myriad of challenges and subsequent topics, you may wonder how and where to get started. Unfortunately, no easy formula exists, but Proverbs 31 affirms the necessity of and the responsibility to advocate. This text also offers a helpful starting point:

- **OPEN YOUR MOUTH:** Only you can decide when it's appropriate to speak up about an issue. Do you have the time and energy to advocate? How much knowledge or advocacy experience do you have? If the answers to these questions are "no" and "not very much," consider supporting or joining an existing effort. You may also want to think about the following questions:

    1. What topics or issues are important to you and why?
    2. What new perspective do you bring to the conversation on this issue? Take a look at what local, state, and national organizations say. Do you agree or disagree?

3. What message would you like to convey?
4. Who is your target audience?

If you, a family member, or a caregiver are advocating about a personal issue, documenting previous attempts to resolve the issue through other means can be extremely important in creating a case. Keeping a record of others' behaviors or responses can also be helpful if you need to recount the details and timeline of an incident. Understanding your options for voicing concerns can be helpful in determining the best advocacy strategy. Organizations can often discern genuine concerns versus general complaining. If you're going to open your mouth, make sure you have adequate evidence to support and authenticate your concern.

JUDGE RIGHTEOUSLY: Some people look for any opportunity to bring a lawsuit in hopes of either making a name for themselves or receiving a financial settlement. This should not be your reason for pursuing a particular issue. Such motivations impact your witness as a believer and do not reflect the righteous character that God desires from his children. If you're struggling to make a case because no strong supporting evidence exists, you may want to rethink raising the concern. Misrepresenting a situation for your own financial gain never ends well. If you're going to bring up an issue, make sure it fits squarely within existing guidance.

DEFEND THE RIGHTS OF THE POOR AND NEEDY: This portion of Proverbs 31:9 reminds us to consider the rights of others as we advocate. Even if you are among those who are impacted by an issue, your goal should never be to benefit yourself alone, but also to speak for those who don't have the ability or the means to advocate for themselves. As a reminder, even when you advocate for yourself, you speak on behalf of those who have gone before you and those who will come after you.

Advocacy can be difficult and exhausting work. Doing the right thing often is. And knowing where to start can be just as challenging. Scroll through any social media platform or peruse recent news feeds, and you'll quickly find a dozen ways the world is messed up and in need of healing.

The good news is, fixing all that brokenness is not on you alone. When you join in the work of advocacy, you join so many other voices already engaged in this mission. More than that, you join the work of God's justice in the world. Which means you don't need to rely solely on your own strength, knowledge, or energy. God will equip you to do his good work. You simply need to step out in faith, draw on his strength, and use your voice in the unique way he has called you to.

LORD, *thank you that we have an advocate in the Holy Spirit. Please help me to advocate in a way that honors you and benefits those who may come after me. Please help me be slow to anger and quick to resolve issues before they escalate. I don't want to feel like I have a chip on my shoulder, but I also don't want to be fearful of opening my mouth. Lord, give me the courage to advocate on my own when necessary. Bring people around me who know how to properly advocate, so that I can grow in this skill. Thank you, Lord, that you defend the rights of those who are marginalized or unable to speak for themselves. Help me be that type of person.*

IN JESUS'S NAME, *Amen.*

Share Your Story

PROMPT: What disability issues pique your interest? If you're unsure, consider an area where you've personally experienced challenges.

ACTION STEP: Take some time to learn about what other advocates may be doing to advance disability rights in your area of interest. Consider how you can get involved or support their existing efforts.

FOR LOVED ONES AND CAREGIVERS: What issues are important to you as a caregiver, family member, or friend? Take some time to consider how you can support and advance advocacy efforts in these areas. This may include offering financial support, participating in national efforts to raise awareness (e.g., signing up for a ten-kilometer run), or posting information on social media.

FOR PASTORS AND CHURCH LEADERS: In what ways has your church been involved in advocacy efforts in the community? Are there additional ways you can encourage members of your congregation to advocate for the needs of people with disabilities and other underserved or underrepresented groups?

DAY 17

Being Transformed by the Journey

ENDURING THE REFINEMENT PROCESS

In this you rejoice, though now for a little while, if necessary, you have been grieved by various trials, so that the tested genuineness of your faith—more precious than gold that perishes though it is tested by fire—may be found to result in praise and glory and honor at the revelation of Jesus Christ.

1 Peter 1:6–7

BLACKMAIL, unreported sexual abuse, and clear power plays. I felt like I had stumbled upon a Hollywood movie set. I kept reminding myself, *This is my church's membership meeting*. It almost didn't seem real. That night, I witnessed the first cracks that led to the crumbling of my church family—one I had grown to love for six years.

In the days, weeks, and years that followed, the depth and breadth of devastation remained incomprehensible. News of assertions and denials, divorces, and individuals deconstructing their faith (including some of the most senior leaders) continue to this day.

Although I remained at the church for several more years following those events, being actively involved proved incredibly difficult, as friends and pastors went their separate ways. Given the emotional and spiritual toll I began to feel, as well as the ongoing aftershocks I experienced, I eventually started avoiding in person services entirely. That didn't change until 2018, when Mathew and I moved to Florida.

With some time and distance now separating me from that damaging church experience, I've come to realize that perfect closure or resolution will be unlikely to happen this side of Heaven. I've made peace with that reality, but faint scars remain. Even so, I can say without question that God used those trials to strengthen my love for Jesus and for his church.

All of us will encounter challenges that will cause us to question God's sovereignty and calling in our lives. Many of Jesus's early followers likely dealt with similar struggles. But the early verses of 1 Peter 1 remind us that God is not surprised by trials and hardships. In fact, he ordains particular trials for us. Often he uses them to strengthen us and bring glory to his name.

If you're like me, you may ask, "Why would a loving God specifically design trials for me?" I get it, friend. At first glance, it seems a bit strange.

Take a closer look, though. Hope is sprinkled in verses 2–9, which explain how God desires to make us more like himself. Even though we deserve death, God demonstrates his mercy by causing us to be "born again."

In our spiritual family, we have access to an inheritance that doesn't fade. The trials we face this side of Heaven may result in questions, fears, and doubts, but God is preparing an inheritance for us and guarding each of us to make sure nothing jeopardizes our inheritance. Paul reiterated the same idea in Romans 8:35: "Who shall separate us from the love of Christ? Shall trouble or hardship or persecution or famine or nakedness or danger or sword?" Do you notice the word at the beginning of that question? Paul did not ask *what* shall separate us, but *who* shall separate us? (verses 37–38) We are in a spiritual battle, but if we are securely in God's hands, no person or spiritual power can separate us from his love.

In biblical times, the only method for testing gold's purity involved heating it by fire. Although gold melts at 1947°F (1064°C), it does not burn. In other words, there is no chemical change, only a physical change. When gold is heated at high temperatures, all the impurities rise to the top, and a goldsmith can scrape them off. Real gold does not become milky or darkened when exposed to fire. It actually shines more brightly. Once the goldsmith can see his reflection, he can be assured of the gold's purity. More advanced methods of testing gold's purity exist today, but fire still serves as a primary method.

So the next time you're facing hardships that seem endless, remember that your faith is more valuable than gold. Whatever you're facing is not meant to break you but to refine you. Maybe you're experiencing challenges at church, frustrations in your friendships, or difficulties at home due to your disability. If so, I'm so sorry, friend. Those things break God's heart, too. But he can use that hardship for his good purposes, which always include making you more like him.

You may question God's goodness and sovereignty during a hard season. That's completely understandable. From a human perspective, it's logical to think that way. There's only one small "problem": God's ways are different. If you've placed your faith in Christ and his work on the cross for you, the Holy Spirit's presence in your life and your inheritance in Heaven serve as reminders that this life's trials are not the end of your story. Nor are they an accurate reflection of God's love for you.

LORD, *help me rejoice during my suffering and trials, knowing that my inheritance with you is far greater than anything I can gain on earth. Show me what it means to truly rejoice in suffering in a way that brings you glory and honor. Remind me that you are protecting me, and your work will be made complete. I will not be snatched out of your hands. Thank you for bringing me into your family through the ultimate sacrifice of your Son.*

IN JESUS'S NAME, *Amen.*

Share Your Story

PROMPT: Take some time to journal about a recent challenging season, noting areas of struggle as well as encouragement. Identify the truths you've learned and consider how you have put them into practice, or how you plan to do so.

ACTION STEP: Imagine you're putting on the armor of God, as described in Ephesians 6. As you take up your sword and shield, what truth do you need to remember most? Take some time to draw the armor of God or find a picture online. On each piece of the armor, write Scripture or strategies for reminding yourself of the armor you have on today.

FOR LOVED ONES AND CAREGIVERS: Consider ways to encourage and strengthen the loved one or client you serve, particularly as they go through times of more intense struggle. Take some time to pray for them today, and ask the Lord for unique opportunities to come alongside them.

FOR PASTORS AND CHURCH LEADERS: Brainstorm strategies to support those going through trials by reminding them of God's truth and nearness. What can you do to better prepare the congregation for seasons of intense trial?

DAY 18

Hope in the Waiting

TRUSTING GOD'S TIMING

Be still before the LORD and wait patiently for him;
fret not yourself over the one who prospers in his way,
over the man who carries out evil devices!

Psalm 37:7

"I WANT TO WAIT." My resolve increased as the words left my lips. "I'm not ready for another service dog."

Tullis, my first service dog, had retired only two months earlier. Although he was enjoying retirement at my parents' home, I found his absence far more difficult than I'd anticipated. After all, we had spent every day together for six years, and he had measurably impacted my life.

He impressed people with his practical skills, such as retrieving items, opening and closing doors, and turning on and off lights. But his intangible skills were what had profoundly changed me. His class-clown personality frequently "broke the ice" and served as a conversation starter with friends and strangers alike. Perhaps most importantly, he gave me confidence to advocate for myself.

Before I could fully explain my reasons for waiting to get a successor dog, my younger brother, Nabeel, weighed in.

"I'm just not sure how I feel about you living in Washington, DC, without a service dog." He paused, as he considered some of the implications. "If you don't get a successor dog, that means you'll have to wait hours for help picking up dropped items, like your phone. Also, who will assist you with elevator buttons?"

Many of the same questions had already crossed my mind. Still, I felt like if I got another dog so soon, I'd be betraying Tullis. In the end, I waited for more than a year before applying for another service dog. In that time, I encountered several reminders about waiting that may be helpful, whether you're waiting on something tangible like a service animal or health insurance preapproval or something intangible like an apology or physical healing:

REMEMBER WHO YOU ARE WAITING ON AND WHOSE YOU ARE: In seasons of waiting, the enemy seizes the opportunity to stir up doubts about God's goodness and faithfulness. You might feel a powerful urge to intervene and force a change but remember who you are waiting on. Your Father is not someone who promises something then forgets or changes his mind. He is faithful to his word. Instead of trying to push forward in your own strength, ask him for the grace to wait, resting in his promises. Recall that you are a child of the Living God, the one who created everything in the universe. He is actively working on your behalf. Think of it like this: When a dog is commanded to "wait," it fixes its gaze on its master. Based on the dog's knowledge of its master and previous interactions, the dog trusts that its master has something good planned next. In the same way, fix your gaze on God, knowing that he loves you and has something good in store for you.

RECALL WHAT HE HAS DONE: When you feel discouraged, actively call to mind all that God has already done for you. This isn't just a mental exercise; it's a spiritual one. By remembering his past faithfulness, you can strengthen your soul and find the courage to keep going.

Consider starting a simple list. Jot down every instance you can remember when God showed up for you. Keep this list by your bed or on your desk and read it whenever you feel your hope fading. Recalling his past actions in your life will remind you that he is unchanging and will be faithful again.

RECOGNIZE THE WORK HE IS DOING: Sometimes, a season of waiting is a season of preparation. A new job, for example, often requires new skills and training. In the same way, God may be using this time to prepare you for what's to come. This waiting period is not wasted time;

The 504 Sit-In

Section 504 of the Rehabilitation Act of 1973, which prohibits discrimination of people with disabilities in programs and activities that receive federal funds, sparked protests in April 1977. Although it had been signed into law in 1973, implementation and enforcement lagged woefully behind, impacting access to "things like libraries, transportation services, schools, etc."

On April 5, 1977, people with disabilities "staged a sit-in protest in San Francisco [and other cities] to demand greater accessibility and accommodations" for disabled individuals. Known as the 504 Sit-In, the majority of protests lasted one day.

However, in San Francisco, more than 150 disabled people entered the Department of Health, Education, and Welfare (HEW) Federal Building and refused to leave for two weeks despite officials "cutting off food, water, medicine, and more," as well as issuing threats of arrest and eviction. The disabled protesters worked closely with a wide range of allied organizations and individuals, some of whom provided "food, medicine, blankets, and more" to protesters.

After two weeks, the San Francisco protesters traveled to Washington, DC, to intensify efforts against the then Secretary of Health, Education, and Welfare James Califano, Jr. In total, the protest in San Francisco lasted twenty-eight days before the secretary signed and implemented the law. It laid the foundation for the Americans with Disabilities Act in 1990.[28]

it's a classroom. He is intentionally equipping you with the skills and character traits you'll need for the next season of your life.

REMEMBER THAT GOD DOESN'T PUT YOUR ENTIRE LIFE ON HOLD. While you may be waiting in one area, he is often working and leading in others. Ask him to show you where he is moving. He might be inviting you to take up a new hobby, go back to school, or invest in a different relationship. If you're anything like me, it's tempting to equate waiting with wasted time. Nothing could be further from the truth. The Creator of time knows the preciousness of every millisecond, and he's always working.

Waiting on the Lord is not for the faint of heart. But in those moments that are most difficult, remind yourself that you're not simply and randomly waiting. You are waiting on your Heavenly Father who loves and cares for you. He will not abandon you in the waiting. Rather, he will wait with you and continue moving you forward in ways you may not always see.

LORD, *forgive me for the times I have allowed my circumstances to eclipse the steadfast truth of your love and faithfulness. When the waiting feels long and the answers are unclear, help me remember that your mercies are new every morning: a constant source of hope in my pain. Strengthen my trust in your timing and your character, and remind me that your love for me never ceases.*

IN JESUS'S NAME, *Amen.*

Share Your Story

PROMPT: Think back to a season of waiting in your life—a time when you were hoping for a breakthrough, a change, or an answer that felt delayed. What emotions did you experience most powerfully, and why? Describe a specific moment when you felt either a profound sense of God's presence or a deep feeling of his absence. Can you share what was happening in that moment?

ACTION STEP: Take some time to meditate on Lamentations 3:22–23. How do you see the Lord's steadfastness in your life, even amid challenges? Identify one way you can choose to trust in his timing and faithfulness.

FOR LOVED ONES AND CAREGIVERS: When the person you care for experiences a season of health-related uncertainty, what are some practical ways you can demonstrate the Lord's steadfast love and faithfulness?

FOR PASTORS AND CHURCH LEADERS: How have you seen the Lord's steadfast love and faithfulness in your life, your family, or your church? What strategies or lessons did you learn through that experience? Consider sharing your story with someone who may need some encouragement today.

DAY 19

Cherishing the Less-Traveled Path

APPRECIATING YOUR DISTINCT JOURNEY

But you are a chosen race, a royal priesthood,
a holy nation, a people for his own possession,
that you may proclaim the excellencies of him
who called you out of darkness into his marvelous light.

1 Peter 2:9

SO OFTEN STORIES AND CONVERSATIONS related to disability highlight the myriad challenges we face on a regular basis, including inaccessible housing, discrimination, and inequities in employment among other things. What's less well-known or understood are the benefits of living with a disability. That's right, I said it: *benefits.* Membership (in the disability community) has its privileges.

We often experience these benefits when we're able to avoid longer airport lines, find accessible parking close by, not pay for garage parking at certain airports, or secure better seats at concerts or live shows. In fact, I often try to make light of situations that place me on a privileged level, even if it requires me to be separated from my family and friends.

But I get it. Being treated a "special way" doesn't always feel special. Sometimes living with a disability becomes like a weight that is too heavy to bear for even one second longer. Ignorance, inaccessibility, the seeming complexity of even the simplest task, and the desire for a different life can often lead to weariness, bitterness, envy, and despair. I understand all too well, friend. If you're feeling separated or excluded because your life doesn't conform to societal "norms" or expectations, be encouraged with this reminder. God separates his children from the world so we can be included in something far greater: a life in him—an eternal inheritance. And while the world may identify you in only one way, God sees you completely. Seize hold of that truth as you press forward in living in a manner that reflects your identity as God's prized possession.

In 1 Peter 2:9, Peter sought to encourage Christians facing persecution by reminding them of their identity in Christ. He called them "a chosen race, a royal priesthood, a holy nation, a people for his own possession." This was a divinely ordained identity the people didn't choose—and we still don't choose today. It transcends race, nationality, and society's labels. And this membership in the body of Christ definitely comes with its privileges.

But what about your regular life and work? Does your "membership" in the disability community feel more like a burden than a blessing? Some days, it certainly can feel like the former. But try to see where God has uniquely placed you from his perspective. What are some of the unique ways God has blessed you that reflect how you're part of "a royal priesthood"?

Maybe you've been chosen to be an encourager among your peers in the disability community. Perhaps you've been chosen to work on disability policy at the state level. Perhaps you're making policy changes in your church or community. Whatever unique traits or gifts shine through your life are a gift to the disability community. May they serve as a reminder and an encouragement that what you've experienced this side of Heaven only dimly reflects the splendor that awaits ahead.

LORD, *you endured being separated from your Father on the cross. As a result, we never have to worry about being excluded or cut off from you. Thank you for reminding me who I am in you, and how it frees me from feeling like I have to defend myself or resort to hatred and slander when I feel rejected. Take my life, and help me to be a "chosen advocate" that glorifies you regardless of my circumstances. Thank you for providing a better way to navigate life's hardships and difficulties. Help me to embrace the uniqueness of my life, recognizing it reflects your creativity and love. Remind me that I bring you much joy.*

IN JESUS'S NAME, *Amen.*

Share Your Story

PROMPT: List several positive aspects of your life (i.e., a service dog, a unique professional position, friends from a disability-related camp or event, etc.). How has God used these elements to encourage others and demonstrate his goodness and faithfulness?

ACTION STEP: Ask the Lord how he wants to use your uniqueness (i.e., serving as a camp counselor, educating others about the benefits of service animals, or building accessible websites). As you get clarity, take the first step in pursuing development or using this uniqueness to encourage others.

FOR LOVED ONES AND CAREGIVERS: As you think about caring for a loved one or a client with a disability, what unique opportunities or elements of your life can you share to encourage them and demonstrate the love of Christ? For example, as a caregiver, you may not have a lot of personal time for social activities. However, the flipside is that you have the privilege of getting to know someone in a completely different way than your peers.

FOR PASTORS AND CHURCH LEADERS: Consider strategies for equipping your congregation to see their differences, and even the less-than-desirable aspects of their life, as opportunities to demonstrate the love of Christ to the world around them. Maybe those who spend more time in hospitals or care centers can look for ways to encourage others in those places.

DAY 20

Encountering Fellow Travelers

EMBRACING DIVERSITY

As it is, there are many parts, yet one body. The eye cannot say to the hand, "I have no need of you," nor again the head to the feet, "I have no need of you." On the contrary, the parts of the body that seem to be weaker are indispensable, and on those parts of the body that we think less honorable we bestow the greater honor, and our unpresentable parts are treated with greater modesty, which our more presentable parts do not require. But God has so composed the body, giving greater honor to the part that lacked it.

1 Corinthians 12:20–24

I'VE LOST COUNT of how many times I've been asked, "Have you heard of Joni Eareckson Tada?" I sincerely appreciate the question, but experience has taught me that this inquiry usually comes from those with limited or no experience interacting with people with disabilities. While the person is typically trying to connect on some level, the question often creates a barrier rather than tearing one down. It assumes—on some level—one person's experience could represent the rich and complex tapestry of the entire disability community. It's an assumption that simplifies a person, reducing their multifaceted identity to a single, shared trait. We all are susceptible to this pitfall when we attempt to categorize and understand people in our lives.

This is precisely why the biblical metaphor of the body of Christ is so foundational and revolutionary. It teaches us that our unity in faith doesn't erase our individuality; it requires it. Paul's message in 1 Corinthians 12 was a profound rebuke to our human tendency to form homogenous groups and hierarchies. He insisted that every member—with their unique gifts, backgrounds, and even their visible and invisible disabilities—was not just welcome, but absolutely indispensable. "The eye cannot say to the hand, 'I have no need of you,'" he wrote, "nor again the head to the feet, 'I have no need of you.'" In fact, Paul went a step further, asserting that the seemingly weaker or less honorable body parts were actually necessary, and that we should show them even greater honor. This powerful teaching directly confronts the ableist attitudes that often permeate society and, sadly, the church. It reminds us that God designed us for interdependence, not for a system where a few "strong" members care for the "weak."

True belonging for people with disabilities is forged in and through interdependence. It is a profound shift from a charity-based model, where people with disabilities are seen as passive recipients of care, to a community where everyone is an active and necessary contributor. In the body of Christ, a person who uses a wheelchair isn't simply someone to be helped; they are a brother or sister whose unique perspective on perseverance or reliance on God enriches the entire community's faith. A nonverbal member might possess a powerful gift of presence that speaks volumes without a single word. Their very existence in the community challenges our assumptions about what it means to be a "valuable" member of society. This mutual reliance creates a deep sense of belonging that a simple program of inclusion can never achieve. When we are all leaning on and supporting one another, demonstrating a profound love that transcends physical or social divides, we are truly embodying Christ.

In a world fractured by racial, political, and cultural divisions, a unified, diverse church offers a compelling vision of what is possible through the gospel. When we intentionally dismantle the walls of hostility that divide humanity, as Jesus did, we become a powerful witness. This means resisting the urge to group people together based on a single characteristic, whether it's a disability, a professional title, or a specific life stage. Every group shares a common trait, but the truth is we are all multifaceted, and we bring our whole selves to each area of our lives. When we forget this or intentionally reject it, we miss the opportunity to experience the fullness of the body of Christ as God intended.

For church leaders, caregivers, and fellow believers, the path to a more inclusive and interdependent community is about seeing people as people first. I've had assistants tell me they have years of experience with "the disabled," and while I appreciate their exposure, I never want anyone to come in assuming they know what's best for me based on their past experience with another person who has a similar condition. Even if people have the same disability, how they practice their faith and engage with the broader church will differ, sometimes significantly. The question for all of us becomes: Can we move beyond our comfort zones and humbly listen to perspectives that are different from our own?

Ultimately, this means cultivating a community that acknowledges unique gifts and values every person as a co-laborer in the gospel. It means moving past the transactional relationship of helper and helped and into a profound partnership where we all discover our place and purpose. The analogy of the body highlights that when one part suffers, the whole body suffers. Conversely, when one part is honored, the whole body rejoices. This underscores the importance of solidarity, mutual support, and collective advocacy within and with the disability community.

If the thought of meeting the needs of disabled people around you feels like too big a task, remember to take it one step at a time, one relationship at a time. The disability community has so much to offer the church, and vice versa. Let's not miss the opportunity to learn from one another and to demonstrate the love and power of the Gospel to a watching world.

***LORD,** thank you for the diversity of your children, including those with disabilities. Help us learn from one another and build up the body in a way that speaks to the watching world the value of each person. Lord, please give me wisdom about how not only to engage, but also to draw in those with disabilities. And, please give those with disabilities, their families, and caregivers a place to belong. Remove any hostility or misconceptions that would cause division and create barriers to reaching and drawing in the disability community. Please give me friendships and relationships that reflect the dignity and worth of all people. And help my church shift from simply being inclusive to having more of a belonging atmosphere, where we long to be with our brothers and sisters, no matter their ability or background.*

***IN JESUS'S NAME,** Amen.*

Share Your Story

PROMPT: As a person with a disability, how have your own thoughts about disability and the disability community impacted your interaction with people who have different disabilities than you? How can you expand your circle of engagement within the disability community?

ACTION STEP: Get to know other people with disabilities in your community, either by connecting with other churches or community-based disability organizations (i.e., Centers for Independent Living). From your perspective, after talking with people, how can your church enhance outreach to the disability community? What role could you play in spearheading such an initiative?

FOR LOVED ONES AND CAREGIVERS: Consider some differences and similarities between you and your loved one or client. How have both the similarities and differences strengthened your relationship? What lessons have you learned as a result of your relationship and interaction?

FOR PASTORS AND CHURCH LEADERS: Consider strategies to increase appreciation for diversity within your church family. If your church doesn't currently have much diversity, consider ways to increase diversity.

Beyond the Letter of the Law: Applying the Americans with Disabilities Act to Religious Organizations

While the Americans with Disabilities Act, a landmark civil rights law, increased access for people with disabilities in all aspects of American life, its application to religious organizations remains nuanced.

Religious entities—including places of worship and their related schools or programs—are granted a broad exemption. Unlike other public-serving entities, such as businesses and nonprofits, faith-based organizations are not required to meet federal standards, even when engaging in nonreligious activities (e.g., running a private school or hosting a public neighborhood festival). In these instances, the law respects the autonomy of churches and other faith-based organizations.

A faith-based organization with fifteen or more employees must follow federal regulations, which prohibit discrimination against qualified applicants with disabilities. But the Constitution prevents government interference with a church's selection of its spiritual leaders (i.e., those performing essential religious duties).

When it comes to the physical church building, if a third-party entity (e.g., a state polling place, private daycare center, community theater, etc.) rents church space, that entity (as the tenant) must ensure the space is accessible under Title II (state and local governments) or Title III. In such cases, the physical space becomes a shared concern.

Although churches may be technically exempt from federal regulations, many voluntarily comply as a welcoming gesture. They understand that even partial compliance—fixing what can easily be accomplished without significant expense, sends a powerful message to the disability community.

Ultimately, removing a physical barrier is a spiritual act. By choosing accessibility over exemption, a congregation transforms a building into a true sanctuary for all.

Traveling with Others

The Importance of Fellowship

DAY 21

Experiencing Joy on the Journey

CULTIVATING GRATITUDE IN UNCERTAINTY

[G]ive thanks in all circumstances;
for this is the will of God in Christ Jesus for you.

1 Thessalonians 5:18

PLANNING A DESTINATION WEDDING in Maui from Maryland meant I hadn't seen the venue in person. One thing I knew for certain: The website pictures looked nothing like our view as we drove to the venue for rehearsal. Paved roads gave way to gravel, as the manicured lawns became overgrown vegetation. The ocean views shifted into scenes of a dilapidated town, its streets lined with cars in desperate need of repair.

Had I been scammed? Was the whole wedding going to be a bust?

I desperately looked for a silver lining. "Well, at least we're in Maui," I said to Mathew and my sister, who had joined us to check out the venue.

Even though no one uttered a word, I knew the same thought crossed each of our minds: *I hope the venue looks nothing like this.*

When our GPS indicated we had arrived, I searched for any sign of oceanfront but found none. Only a few palm trees dotted the area.

We approached a plain wooden fence with the gate slightly open. My sister and I glanced at each other. *Was this really the place?* She quickly got out of the car and pushed open the gate.

Paradise!

We were speechless. Perfect palm trees waved their fronds, framed by the clear, bright blue sky. The green blanket of grass met the ocean on the horizon. It was more beautiful than I could've ever imagined or hoped for.

Immediately, I thought, *God, why do I always assume the worst when I experience uncertainty on the path you lay before me?*

What about you, friend? Can you relate? When you face the unknown in regard to your health, your job, your relationship, or any area of your life, is your default position questioning and concern or gratitude and hope?

Researchers agree that a common psychological phenomenon, known as "negativity bias," places more emphasis on negative memories and experiences.[29] We are hardwired to spend more time focusing on the negative to reduce the likelihood of loss or pain.

You may wonder, like me, *If I'm hardwired to focus on the negative, how can I possibly cultivate joy amid uncertainty?*

To grow in joy, we must first understand its nature. Joy is not the same as happiness. Happiness is often dictated by our circumstances and, as a result, can be a fleeting emotion. In contrast, joy, as a fruit of the Spirit, is rooted in a relationship with God and the power of his unchanging promises. Because God is constant, our joy can be, too. The world's ever-present uncertainty can potentially rob you of joy and certainly of happiness, especially if you're basing your happiness on material things, external circumstances, or your own ability. But when you base your joy in God, not even disappointments, hardships, or changing circumstances can lessen it. Cultivating joy during a season of uncertainty reorients your heart and mind and helps you more fully recognize the work of God in and through the people and circumstances around you.

If you're unsure how to cultivate joy amid uncertainty, consider the following strategies:

- **SPEND TIME WITH GOD AND IN HIS WORD:** When reading the Bible or enjoying a quiet time with God, avoid the temptation to quickly move on to the next task. As you devote yourself to deepening your relationship with God and better knowing his character, your joy will increase.

- **PRAISE GOD:** Play praise and worship music and sing. Singing can often be a tool to help us shift our thinking from current circumstances to the truth of God's character and sovereignty over our lives.

- **PRACTICE GRATITUDE:** Thankfulness can shift our focus from what we lack to what we have. Making a practice of thanking God for his provision is a way of acknowledging his goodness.

- **BE GENEROUS:** You can be generous with your time, your love for others, and your acts of service. These purposeful activities can help shift your focus away from yourself and toward others. You play a part in and witness all God is doing in the body of Christ.

- **ASK:** You can simply ask for the gift of joy, as John 16:24 suggests. It may seem simplistic, but the Lord loves childlike faith.

When facing the unknown, it's easy to focus on what could go wrong, but we have a greater truth to lean on. Just as my Maui venue was a hidden paradise behind an unremarkable gate, God often hides his greatest blessings just beyond a season of uncertainty. Cultivating joy in the unknown isn't about ignoring the difficulties; it's about intentionally choosing to trust in God's character and his promises, which are unwavering. This shift in focus allows you to find peace that isn't dependent on your circumstances and to recognize the good he is doing, even when the path ahead isn't perfectly clear.

LORD, *thank you that in times of uncertainty, I don't need to be fearful or pessimistic. Even though researchers say that humans are hardwired to respond negatively to uncertainty, your Word reminds me that I am yours, and you can change me. Holy Spirit, I ask that you would transform my heart and mind to see the blessings of God in nature, my friendships, and other areas of my life and environment. May I purposefully choose to praise you even in the uncertainty.*

IN JESUS'S NAME, *Amen.*

Share Your Story

PROMPT: Recall a specific time when you faced significant uncertainty. What were the actions you took to navigate that period? Looking back, what specific aspects of your approach were most effective, and what would you do differently today to better support yourself?

ACTION STEP: To apply what you've learned, start a "Joy Journal." When you encounter Scripture, a quote, or a topic from a podcast that resonates with you, jot it down along with a sentence about why it speaks to you. What is one specific entry you would make today, and why is it particularly meaningful?

FOR LOVED ONES AND CAREGIVERS: As a caregiver, how do you actively manage the uncertainty that comes with supporting a loved one or client? How has witnessing their feelings of uncertainty reshaped your own perspective on the unknown? Reflect on a past time of personal uncertainty and describe one key lesson you learned that has helped you become a more resilient and compassionate caregiver today.

FOR PASTORS AND CHURCH LEADERS: What specific, proactive steps have you taken to equip your congregation to navigate periods of uncertainty? Think beyond general sermons—what practical tools, teachings, or community-building initiatives have been or would be beneficial?

DAY 22

Inviting Others into Your Story

BEING VULNERABLE

A friend loves at all times, and a brother is born for adversity.

Proverbs 17:17

OVER THE COURSE OF SEVERAL WEEKS, a friend in my Bible study mentioned repeatedly that she felt I shouldn't have to navigate my ongoing personal assistant challenges alone. I questioned why she felt so strongly about it. I pridefully thought, *Don't you think I can handle this on my own?* The truth: I certainly needed help, but the thought of being vulnerable scared me.

She mentioned connecting me with her friend, Charlene, who had experience in this area. I didn't know Charlene personally, but I had heard she'd done an excellent job of coordinating care for a gentleman in my church. Still, I doubted the usefulness of talking with her. To appease my friend, I ultimately agreed to a meeting with Charlene.

To my pleasant surprise, Charlene graciously and patiently asked pointed questions about my past experiences, family, present situation, and future considerations. Given her previous professional roles as a nurse manager (head nurse) of an intensive care unit, step-down unit, and later the director of operations for an urgent care clinic, Charlene knew the right questions to ask and understood the common home health-care issues.

The conversation and Charlene herself were an answer to prayer. By the end of our initial discussion, we had outlined a three-stage plan: bring my current staff level up, develop a pool of full-in staff, and address some related issues (i.e., inconsistent care and some accessibility challenges in my condominium). Over the next few months, Charlene and I developed a strong friendship that still exists today.

According to the U.S. Centers for Disease Control and Prevention, social isolation and loneliness remain a significant threat to mental and physical health. One in three adults report feeling lonely, while one in four don't have social and emotional support. Social isolation refers to the contact or relationships a person has, while loneliness refers to a feeling of disconnectedness or a lack of meaningful relationships. Disability and health issues as well as environmental factors (e.g., lack of transportation, lack of access to services and support living in a rural area) serve as risk factors for isolation, loneliness, and health concerns.[30]

Regardless of your relationship or experience with disability, remember that people with disabilities, their families, caregivers, and other supporters desire and need genuine, meaningful friendships like everyone else—not relationships based on pity. An attitude of pity creates an unspoken hierarchy that frequently views a person with a disability as being in a lower position or not having as much to give. This creates an imbalance in the relationship. On the other hand, sibling-like relationships in the body of Christ are often born out of difficult circumstances. These types of relationships are beneficial, because the person with a disability is loved and cared for from a place of genuine love and affection.

Research shows that healthy friendships can often help you navigate life's challenges while reducing the likelihood of negative impacts due to life's uncertainties.[31] Here are a few things to keep in mind when building friendships:

- **FOR INDIVIDUALS WITH DISABILITIES:** When it comes to building friendships and social connections, consider taking the initiative, as many people may feel hesitant to interact. Making the first move or gently letting someone know what you need can be a great relief, and sharing your story when you feel safe can help others understand you better and build trust. Remember also to acknowledge your own limits. A meaningful friendship doesn't have to be a big, demanding commitment, but can instead start with a short phone call or a few minutes of conversation. Consider the types of accommodations you normally need and come prepared. For example, you may want to consider leaving a portable ramp at someone's house, so you can attend Bible study on a regular basis.

FOR LOVED ONES AND CAREGIVERS: You play a vital role in supporting your loved one's social life and in maintaining your own. You can be a bridge by modeling natural, respectful interactions and creating opportunities for your loved one to connect with others. It's also important to be honest with others about your time and energy constraints. A good first step in building a relationship may be to schedule a virtual coffee or phone call or even arrange to meet a few minutes before or after a Sunday service, which reduces the need for additional transportation.

FOR PASTORS AND CHURCH LEADERS: As the shepherd of your community, you have the power to shape a culture of genuine, Christ-like friendship. You can help by intentionally raising awareness through sermons and volunteer training to address the common fears people have about interacting with disabled people and making sure they are seen as a vital part of the body of Christ. Be mindful that the traditional "meet and greet" may not be accessible for everyone, so create opportunities for flexible, low-energy social options like virtual Bible studies or prayer groups.

We are not meant to live the Christian life alone. Your story and unique experiences make you an important part of the body of Christ. Seeking creative ways to connect is a powerful step in building biblical friendships.

Caregivers and loved ones, your call to community is just as important. As you love and serve others, may you also experience grace in seeking out connections that honor your unique circumstances.

And to pastors and church leaders, you have a sacred opportunity to cultivate a culture where every member feels seen, valued, and deeply connected.

Let us all, together, commit to fostering these friendships that reflect the love of Christ and strengthen us all for the journey ahead.

> ***LORD,*** *thank you so much that I am built for relationship. Thank you for the people you've brought into my life to encourage me, change me, and help me grow in my faith and love for you. I am especially grateful for friends who have come alongside me during hard and dark seasons of life. Thank you for the deep friendships that are born out of those experiences. Please bless my friends today, and please help me know how I can bless them through my words and actions. Help me encourage my friends today, and I ask that you bring new friends across my path.*
>
> ***IN JESUS'S NAME,*** *Amen.*

Share Your Story

PROMPT: Describe a friendship that has significantly impacted your life. What core qualities did that person embody, and how did their actions demonstrate those qualities? Why are these specific traits non-negotiable for you in a healthy friendship?

ACTION STEP: This week, reach out to one friend and specifically thank them for a way they've invested in your life. As you reflect on their friendship, think of one tangible way their example has inspired you to be a more supportive and present friend to others.

FOR LOVED ONES AND CAREGIVERS: Amid your caregiving responsibilities, how have you intentionally prioritized connection with a close friend? If this has been a challenge, what is one small, manageable step you could take this week to reconnect with someone who supports you?

FOR PASTORS AND CHURCH LEADERS: How do you intentionally demonstrate and teach the principles of healthy, biblical friendship to your congregation? What specific practices or initiatives have been most effective, and what is one new step you are considering to further cultivate a culture of deep, supportive friendship within your church?

DAY 23

Sharing Your Divinely Given Gifts

STRENGTHENING THE BODY

Having gifts that differ according to the grace given to us,
let us use them: if prophecy, in proportion to our faith; if service,
in our serving; the one who teaches, in his teaching;
the one who exhorts, in his exhortation; the one who contributes,
in generosity; the one who leads, with zeal;
the one who does acts of mercy, with cheerfulness.

Romans 12:6–8

"HELLO! WELCOME! I'm so glad you're here. Come on in and make yourself at home. You can put those brownies in the kitchen."

I waited near the door and greeted each person as more friends arrived for the evening's Bible study. As my home filled with the sound of voices and laughter, I felt a surge of joy in my chest. I silently thanked God for allowing me to share my home and my heart with all these amazing people.

One of my great joys is hosting and making others feel welcome, sheltered, and safe. Honing my spiritual gift of hospitality definitely didn't happen overnight, though. I had to go through a lot of trial and error and creative thinking before I learned to embrace this gift in all its fullness.

When you come to faith, the Holy Spirit gives you a divine gift to build up the body of Christ. But how do you know that the Holy Spirit is at work in your life? The Holy Spirit's work may come through what is commonly referred to as the fruit of the Spirit, or outward evidence of the Spirit's work in you: "But the fruit of the Spirit is love, joy, peace, patience, kindness, goodness, faithfulness, gentleness, self-control" (Galatians 5:22–23). These attributes indicate that the Holy Spirit is present and working in a believer's life.

As described throughout the Bible, spiritual gifts are meant to build up, encourage, and strengthen others in the body of Christ. They should not be used to tear others down, dismiss serving opportunities in other areas, or boast when talking to someone else. First and foremost, these are gifts, which means we do nothing to deserve them and can't even use them on our own strength or power. In many cases, a person may need to grow into their spiritual gifts, but these gifts may also build upon existing or learned skills and talents.

No matter what physical, emotional, or social limitations you might have to face each day, you can use your unique and God-given gifts to love and bless others. Maybe you are a skilled listener, someone whose quiet and steady presence provides comfort and encouragement to those around you. If that's you, love by listening. Or maybe you're a gifted speaker or teacher. If that's you, you have been beautifully blessed to use your voice to educate and build up those in your community, perhaps as an advocate or spiritual mentor.

As you discern what your unique gifting from God might be, consider the following points:

- **EXAMINE:** What fills your heart with joy as you interact with others? Do people often come to you with similar requests for prayer, wisdom, or guidance? Is there something that comes naturally to you? Take some time to sit with God and ask him to help you examine your heart. If it's helpful, take a closer look at the passages that highlight spiritual gifts (1 Corinthians 12:8–10,

28–29; Romans 12:3–8; Ephesians 4:11; and 1 Corinthians 7:7), and consider your inherited skills and talents. Take time to consider the ministries of your church. If you're currently not connected to a church, think about issues or activities that resonate deeply with you.

PRAY: Ask the Lord to help you discern your gift. It may or may not overlap with your natural gifts and talents. Fight the urge to consider your limitations. You can take the opportunity to trust the Lord and step out in faith. The God who uniquely made you will also uniquely equip you.

SERVE: Consider serving with an existing ministry to give you an idea of how you may exercise a particular gift. Use this as an opportunity to really expand and explore your thoughts and ideas related to a particular gift. Don't discount the hidden gifts, such as intercession, faith, and discernment. These can be powerful, extremely meaningful gifts to the church. Keep in mind there may be differences in how a gift is expressed by someone with a disability. For example, hospitality is one of my gifts. However, I have difficulty preparing my home or food for visitors. So, I simply open my home as a potential meeting place for Bible studies and other gatherings and let others provide the snacks.

REFLECT: Write down what you have enjoyed or not enjoyed about a serving experience. It may be worth trying several different ministries, so you can get a broader idea of the types of activities you enjoy. Be willing to share your preferences with church leaders but also recognize that you may be asked to serve in a different capacity, based on the church's needs and ministries. Think about times when you've served or helped others in a spiritual context. When did you feel most effective? When did you see positive results or impact?

- **AFFIRM:** Chances are your gift will be affirmed by those who know you well. Perhaps multiple people have mentioned to you that you have a gift for prayer, generosity, or leadership. Seeking input from trusted friends, family, or ministry leaders is a vital part of discovering your spiritual gift.

Pastors and church leaders play a particularly vital role in helping members of their congregation discover and use spiritual gifts. Although churches and other places of worship are not covered under the Americans with Disabilities Act (ADA), creating an inclusive environment is well worth the investment. This includes actively identifying and removing architectural barriers, communication barriers, and attitudinal barriers. Depending on an individual's disability and the requirements for serving, roles and responsibilities may need to be adjusted.

Given that you know your needs best, have a conversation with your pastor and church leaders about your needs and interests. You may be particularly drawn to ministries that help and serve those in need. You may also have unique perspectives related to perseverance and resilience to share. Think outside the box when it comes to how you can use your skills and experiences to bless others.

In the disability community, there is a motto: Nothing about us, without us. It is often used to talk about involving people with disabilities in policymaking and program activities that impact the community. The same could be said for ministries and activities in the church. If your church has a ministry to help people with disabilities, make sure to involve disabled people in all aspects of that ministry. Avoid tokenism, where people with disabilities are included in outward-facing serving opportunities simply as a means of creating the appearance of being inclusive.

Spiritual gifts come from your Heavenly Father, who is the Maker of the Universe. He knows not only how he made you, but where he placed you. Take some time to discover the gift he has given you for the edification of others and the church.

LORD, *thank you so much for spiritual gifts. Thank you that it's simply another way you seek to bless us and your church when we lay our lives down for you. Lord, I might not even be sure what my spiritual gifts are or how I can use them most for your glory, but I ask that you would give me clear vision and wisdom. Guide me in the way you would have me go. Thank you so much for the gift of the Holy Spirit, who equips and empowers us to do your good work in the world.*

IN JESUS'S NAME, *Amen.*

Share Your Story

PROMPT: How do you believe God has uniquely gifted you for service, and what is one specific way you are using that gift today? If you are still discerning your gift, what is a specific Scripture or prayer you will use this week to seek clarity?

ACTION STEP: This week, reach out to a trusted friend or church leader and ask them to share their observations about your spiritual gifts. What is one specific piece of insight you hope to gain from that conversation?

FOR LOVED ONES AND CAREGIVERS: In what unique and beautiful ways have you observed your loved one or client expressing their spiritual gifts, even if it looks different from traditional expectations? As a caregiver, what specific support or resources from the church would empower you to more effectively use your own spiritual gifts?

FOR PASTORS AND CHURCH LEADERS: What specific, intentional strategies are currently in place to help disabled members of your congregation not only discern their spiritual gifts but also find meaningful opportunities to utilize them? What is one new, practical step your leadership team is considering to further break down barriers and create a more inclusive culture of service?

Serving Others Along the Way

MAKING A DIFFERENCE

"And when did we see you a stranger and welcome you, or naked and clothed you? And when did we see you sick or in prison and visit you?" And the King will answer them, "Truly, I say to you, as you did it to one of the least of these my brothers, you did it to me."

Matthew 25:38–40

SEVERAL YEARS AGO, while serving at a local food distribution event, I approached another volunteer coordinating the setup. Before I completed my question, she looked at my husband and asked, "What is she doing here? There's nothing she can help with."

I resisted the urge to give the woman a piece of my mind. Instead, I moved away from her and did the best I could to find some way to serve. I eventually joined the clothing table to make sure everyone could find the items they needed.

Scripture reminds us that serving is a foundational aspect of the Christian faith. Jesus himself said, "The Son of Man did not come to be served but to serve" (Matthew 20:28). As we are made more like Jesus, we will grow in our desire to emulate his servant heart. When we do, we will be better able to show God's love and the power of the gospel to others in the church as well as to a watching world. At its core, service is a tangible way we participate in God's work in the world.

Serving brings with it a lot of benefits, not only for those being served, but also for those doing the serving. In addition to reducing the burden on church leaders and staff, serving strengthens church unity, creates an outward-focused church culture, and increases the church's effectiveness in achieving its mission. On an individual level, volunteering or serving others has been shown to lower stress, reduce depressive symptoms, and lead to a greater sense of well-being and happiness. Healthy ministries serve as a great means of outreach and compassion by addressing social needs, fostering community growth, and positively influencing a region.

On a very practical level, serving also helps young people and those entering the workforce develop new skills or sharpen existing skills. This practical experience can enhance self-esteem, boost confidence, and further professional development. Such experience can be critical for people with disabilities, who often face barriers to work-based learning opportunities and full-time employment.

Acts of service can take many different forms. Just as each of us has a unique fingerprint, we also have unique ways and methods of serving. In other words, there's no one right or wrong way to serve. So, if you're wondering whether you can serve, the answer is "Absolutely!"

For me, how I've served has changed over the years. I attribute that to life changes and God opening up different opportunities. I've served as part of the communications and counseling teams in a five-thousand-member church. In smaller churches, I've shared my disability expertise with members either navigating disability for the first time or serving people with disabilities in a professional capacity. My home has also served as a location for gatherings and Bible studies. In other seasons, medical issues prevented me from being as involved as I would have liked, and those times have resulted in lots of conversations with God. I've come to recognize that in those seasons, I can pray for others or send letters of encouragement.

Whatever your life looks like right now, trust that the Lord will show you how he wants you to serve in this season. Consider your spiritual gifts and think about ways to use them creatively. If you can't find a place to serve, don't be discouraged. Keep praying and rest on the Lord's promise that he has good plans for you. Also keep in mind that there may be seasons when you need to step back from serving—and that's perfectly fine.

A gentle reminder: Don't believe the lie that not serving somehow puts your faith in question. Some people may point to Scriptures like James 2:17 or 2:26 to support their personal assumptions and assessments. However, looking at these verses in isolation does not allow for an accurate interpretation. We must look at the entire passage: James 2:17–26. Contrary to what some may believe, James is not suggesting that salvation comes through good works. Rather, he is asserting that good works are a natural outcome of genuine faith.

As you consider serving, think about what is on your heart, and what you enjoy doing. Take some time to pray as well. Don't be afraid to ask the Lord what good work he has for you. Remember, serving is just one of the many ways to worship God. Whether you regularly serve on a ministry team, send encouraging words to others, or pray for the church's missionaries, God is honored by your acts of love and worship.

God also understands your heart and the ways he has gifted you. He intimately knows your current abilities and limitations. Any guilt, shame, or external pressure you feel does not reflect the Lord's heart for you. Like the young boy who gave his five loaves and two fish to feed the multitude, Jesus is pleased with any offering we bring. It is not the size of the offering, but the heart behind it that captures his attention. Trust that he has good works prepared for you that will utilize the spiritual gifts and natural abilities he has given you.

LORD, *thank you for allowing us to take part in your mission by serving. Thank you for Jesus's example of true humility and a servant's heart. Please give me wisdom and understanding in knowing how you want me to use my gifts to serve the church, advance your kingdom, and bless my community. Please help me let go of any harmful words or attitudes that have been directed toward me with regard to serving. I confess they have made it difficult to serve at times. Thank you that it is not so much about the size of our gifts, but the heart behind the gift. Would you also bring people across my path who I can befriend and get to know on a deeper level? Help my love for the body of Christ grow as you give me a love for the surrounding communities and wisdom to know how to best serve those I meet.*

IN JESUS'S NAME, *Amen.*

Share Your Story

PROMPT: Reflecting on your unique interests, talents, and skills, what is one specific area of service that you feel a growing sense of passion or "holy dissatisfaction" toward? Describe what this inner "nudge" feels like and why you believe it might be from God.

ACTION STEP: This week, spend focused time in prayer about the area you've identified. Ask for clarity and a clear first step. What is one tangible action, however small, you will take this week to explore this new path of service?

FOR LOVED ONES AND CAREGIVERS: What is one area of service where you have observed your loved one or client truly light up and thrive? What support would your loved one or client need to be successful in a serving role, and what steps could you take to advocate for them? As a caregiver, what specific support or resources would empower you to pursue your own calling to serve?

FOR PASTORS AND CHURCH LEADERS: How have you intentionally created space to listen to disabled members of your congregation about the barriers they face in serving? Based on these conversations, what specific, necessary adjustments have you made, or what new, inclusive serving opportunities have been created? What is one actionable step your church can take this month to make a serving role more accessible?

DAY 25

Encouraging Others

TESTIFYING TO GOD'S FAITHFULNESS

Blessed be the God and Father of our Lord Jesus Christ,
the Father of mercies and God of all comfort, who comforts
us in all our affliction, so that we may be able to comfort those
who are in any affliction, with the comfort with which we ourselves
are comforted by God. For as we share abundantly in Christ's
sufferings, so through Christ we share abundantly in comfort too.

2 Corinthians 1:3–5

ONE AFTERNOON, my assistant asked if I'd be willing to speak to her friend Diana. Diana's daughter, Jackie, was preparing to enter college. Although Jackie used crutches, she only required assistance with some activities of living, including showering, dressing, and cooking. While Diana had been Jackie's sole caregiver up to that point, Jackie needed to transition to hiring and managing her own care.

When I spoke to Diana and Jackie, they explained Jackie's needs and mentioned they had never hired assistants. I shared in detail my own process of becoming more independent in this area.

"Thank you so much for sharing all these resources and ideas," said Jackie, with a deep sense of relief evident in her voice. "It's helpful to know I'm not alone, and there's someone I can talk to who has been through a similar experience."

Over the years, I've had the privilege of sharing many parts of my story through one-on-one conversations, writing, videos, and presentations. I've shared my thoughts and experiences as a church member, as a service dog recipient and handler, as a disability advocate, as a working professional, and as a woman living with a disability. How and what I share depends largely on the audience, the setting, and the topic I've been asked to talk on. Inevitably, as I seek to comfort someone with a story of how God has moved in my life, I also come away encouraged as I remember God's faithfulness.

When I first began sharing my story, I asked myself: *Is my story really worth sharing? Will it truly help anyone?* I've learned in time that the answer to both these questions is a resounding "Yes!"

Whether your story is still unfolding or you've shared your story dozens of times, remember that God can often use your experiences to minister to others. 2 Corinthians 1:3–5 reveals that one way he does this is by comforting us so we can comfort others.

The word "comfort" here is the Greek word παρακαλέω (pronounced *parégoria*), which means to ask for earnestly, to encourage, to exhort. That definition reminds me of Matthew 11:28: "Come to me, all who labor and are heavy laden, and I will give you rest." God invites us—implores us—to come to him, so he can alleviate our fears, worries, sadness, and anxiety. He does this for us, so we can do it for others.

Although God works in each life a little differently, elements of your story will undoubtedly resonate with others, helping to encourage, comfort, or challenge them. Undoubtedly, your testimony speaks powerfully of God's grace and faithfulness amid adversity. At its heart, your story highlights God's kindness and mercy in the ways he has moved in your life.

From a disability perspective, sharing your story also serves as an educational opportunity. It helps break down barriers, especially for those who haven't interacted much with people with disabilities. It serves as a platform for dispelling misconceptions, challenging negative stereotypes, and confronting stigma. Your openness about living with a disability creates a safe space for people to ask questions without feeling awkward or out of place. Since conversations about disability often focus on limitations, sharing your story can provide an opportunity to highlight your unique gifts, talents, and contributions to the community. It may even open doors for additional opportunities to serve within the church.

Most importantly, sharing your story is a wonderful way to tell others about Jesus and to invite them into your world. Vulnerability creates a bond, reveals common ground, and builds unity. Keep in mind, though, that you are not obligated to share your entire story with everyone who asks. You can decide when, where, and how much of your story to share with someone else. You owe no one an explanation. After all, your story is important and special and should only be shared with those who will handle it with care.

LORD, *thank you so much for giving me my story. It is precious in your sight. Use it in whatever way you see fit. It is, after all, a story of your grace, mercy, and redemption. As I share with others, please give me wisdom, discernment, and clarity. Please open doors to the places you'd like me to share, and close doors that are not from you. Help me to share your comfort with those in need. All for your glory, Lord.*

IN JESUS'S NAME, *Amen.*

Share Your Story

PROMPT: As you prepare to share your story, identify one specific part that you feel reluctant to share. What is the core emotion or fear connected to this reluctance? How will you prayerfully approach this part of your story in a way that honors both your vulnerability and the listener's trust?

ACTION STEP: Take time this week to outline your story, focusing on the pivotal moments that shaped you. What is one overarching theme or lesson that connects these moments? Write a single paragraph describing the importance of this theme and what it teaches you about God's faithfulness.

FOR LOVED ONES AND CAREGIVERS: As a caregiver, take some time this week to write out one significant moment from your journey. What specific challenges and encouragements did you experience in that moment? What is one lesson you learned that you can share with another caregiver to help them feel seen and less alone?

FOR PASTORS AND CHURCH LEADERS: What intentional opportunities currently exist within your church for disabled people, their loved ones, or caregivers to share their stories in a safe and dignifying way? If such opportunities are not in place, what is one tangible way you can begin creating a space for these voices to be heard and valued?

Ethical Storytelling: Avoiding the "Overcoming" Narrative

In the church, testifying to God's work through our personal stories has always been a sacred act. Whether the psalmist's cry for deliverance, a quiet conversation with a friend, or the lived experience of disability, every story testifies to God's love and care for his creation. Both sharing and receiving a story involves sacred trust. To handle a story carelessly is to mishandle a life.

Too often, when it comes to stories involving disability, we frame disability as a tragedy to be defeated or a lesson to be learned. When we do this, we risk creating what some in the disability community refer to as "inspiration porn," where the complexity of a person's life simply becomes a tool to motivate, prompt gratefulness, and even inflict guilt. Some disability advocates argue this approach dehumanizes the storyteller by reducing their existence to a single function: inspiring the nondisabled. It hides the real-world barriers and systemic issues that caregivers and loved ones face daily, minimizing the truth that our value is found in whose we are, not in our abilities.

A church that truly welcomes everyone—and one where all feel like they belong—sees every member as necessary. For pastors, families, and individuals, this means embracing one another as co-laborers whose presence makes the body of Christ whole.

Ethical storytelling follows a powerful principle: The person with lived experience is the expert and primary authority on their life—and they should have as much autonomy (and support) as possible to direct all aspects of their life, including how their story is shared. For nondisabled peers, family members, caregivers, and supporters, this translates into making space for stories that are ongoing, complex, or unresolved.

Life this side of heaven is hard. But when we become more vulnerable, we can recognize the value of every voice in serving as a witness to a watching and hurting world, remembering that God has the final word in our story.

Beyond the Horizon

Living Purposefully, Dreaming Boldly

DAY 26

Doing Life Together

BELONGING IN GOD'S FAMILY

A new commandment I give to you, that you love one another:
just as I have loved you, you also are to love one another.
By this all people will know that you are my disciples,
if you have love for one another.

John 13:34–35

I HAD ONLY BEEN ATTENDING the church a few months when I sensed the Holy Spirit leading me to move from downtown Washington, DC, to Rockville, Maryland, forty-five minutes northwest. Although the move increased my work commute by thirty minutes, I knew being closer to the church increased my chances of being more involved and building relationships. I knew without faith and fellowship, my chances of staying in Washington, DC, long-term decreased significantly.

When I shared the news with my small group, they immediately asked how they could help. When moving day arrived, many in the group helped my parents pack up last-minute items and loaded the moving truck. The help didn't stop there. In the first few weeks, as I was still looking for help, both the men and women jumped in to assist me. The ladies spearheaded my personal care while the guys took care of light housekeeping and making things as accessible as possible for me.

My small group's willingness to care for me in practical ways during this transition served as a powerful witness to my family and neighbors.

Connecting with community is a central component of the Christian faith, as essential as prayer and worship. It's a means for demonstrating Christ's love by bearing one another's burdens (Galatians 6:2), rejoicing together, and comforting each other in times of sorrow. Community is where we challenge one another to grow and mature in our faith (Proverbs 27:17). It's also a powerful testament to our unity in Christ, despite our diverse backgrounds and personalities.

The way we connect with others—whether through conversation, shared activities, or offering emotional support—can take many different forms, depending on the type of relationship and the environment. You might have a close friend you engage with weekly or even daily. Or perhaps you have a friend you see only rarely but text or call often. Knowing your attachment style and agreeing on "rules of engagement" with the other person can be helpful in maintaining the relationship bond. But of course, you also need to know the other person's boundaries and be willing to pivot sometimes. As a person with a disability, I consider flexibility and grace one of the greatest demonstrations of love in a friendship.

If you, like me, prefer more intimate social gatherings over large group events or feel discouraged whenever a friendship takes a long time to develop, take heart. God didn't design us all the same way, and we shouldn't fall into the trap of believing there are *right* and *wrong* ways to forge connections. Building a strong community doesn't happen by accident. It requires intentionality and a willingness to step out.

As you look for practical ways to invest in your community, consider some of these options for making deeper connections:

- **DON'T BE AFRAID TO MAKE THE FIRST MOVE:** Many beautiful friendships start with a simple invitation for a coffee or a meal. You could also send a quick text to let someone know you're thinking of them or to extend a personal invitation to join an event or Bible study. Taking initiative demonstrates your openness to welcoming others and fosters a sense of belonging.

OPEN YOUR HOME AND HEART: Being hospitable does not require a grand gesture—even a simple gathering can create lasting memories and strengthen bonds. So even if you're not able to prepare or provide snacks, offer your home as a location for a weekly small group. Oftentimes, the members of the group can bring snacks and drinks and make themselves at home. I typically tell my guests, "I can't reach anything, but I can tell you where everything is." Acknowledging your limitations helps everyone relax and feel comfortable. If accessibility is an issue, try to find a location and time that serves everyone, or utilize a public place that has private rooms, such as a local library.

BE VULNERABLE AND AUTHENTIC: Giving ourselves permission to be vulnerable encourages others to do the same. Such openness leads to profound and lasting connections, because when we allow ourselves to be known by others, we open ourselves to deeper love.

LISTEN ACTIVELY: Listening honors each person's unique story. Active listening demonstrates your genuine interest and care and also helps you understand someone else's perspectives and experiences.

SERVE AND ENCOURAGE: Look for ways to serve and encourage those around you. Send an encouraging note, offer help, or simply be present for someone in need. Serving blesses others and strengthens your connection to the community. It also aligns with Jesus's teaching on being a servant (Mark 10:45).

ESTABLISH HEALTHY BOUNDARIES: Protect your time and energy by not taking on too much and avoiding toxic individuals. A healthy balance in your life and relationships directly impacts your well-being and ability to be fully present for others.

- **SHARE YOUR TESTIMONY:** Sharing your experiences, struggles, and joys makes you more relatable. Your story can encourage others, create a sense of connectedness, and strengthen the bonds of friendship.

- **BE CONSISTENT:** Show up as often as possible for community gatherings, small group meetings, and one-on-one catchups. Consistency demonstrates your commitment to fostering meaningful relationships.

- **HONOR ONE ANOTHER:** Treat one another with respect and honor, valuing each person's unique contributions. Extend grace and compassion rather than making assumptions or judgments. This includes honoring and loving others with whom you might not agree.

- **PARTICIPATE FULLY:** Use every opportunity to get involved. Attend services and events and look for serving opportunities where you can use your spiritual gifts. You will naturally connect with others who share your passions and interests.

- **STAY FOR FELLOWSHIP:** Don't be in a hurry to leave after a service or gathering ends. Many meaningful connections can be made during casual moments. Practice the skill of introducing yourself, asking for someone else's name, and getting to know them. Continue building on existing connections as an investment into the lives of others.

Our capacity for connection shifts with seasons of life. Whether you're in a bustling season of growth, a quiet period of introspection, or in a challenging time of navigating significant difficulties, God can bring connection. If deep connection feels elusive to you right now, pour out your heart before the Lord. He can bring the right people at the proper time.

If you are in a season of more limitations or tighter margins, don't listen to the whispers in your head saying you are not "connecting enough." A social calendar filled to the brim does not earn God's favor. True connection can often be found in deep or quiet moments, in a thoughtful text message, or in a shared moment of vulnerability with a trusted friend. God values your sincere desire to love others, even when circumstances limit your expression of it.

Connecting with community often includes accepting a person's strengths, limitations, and external constraints. Similar to the way families with children may require extra childcare provision or timing flexibility, people with disabilities may also need additional assistance when arranging or spending time together. This could include offering to drive or even going to their home, planning group activities that are both accessible and simple, or checking in via phone calls or texts. When we customize our connections according to each person's individual needs, we are able to show them greater love.

As you consider your connections, focus on what genuinely refreshes your spirit and what you enjoy doing with others. Pray and ask the Lord to reveal the relationships and communities where you can flourish. Remember to honor your boundaries, respecting your own needs and capacities, as you trust in God's perfect timing.

LORD, *thank you for making us for relationships and community. Please remove the fear and anxiety I feel about meeting new people. I want to be able to establish longer-term relationships. Bring people across my path that I can talk to. And when I struggle with feelings of envy, bitterness, or frustration toward others, help me remember that these are my brothers and sisters in Christ. Let me love them well and honor their stories. Help me be an encouragement no matter how I might be feeling personally. Give me the courage and the ability to continue showing up.*

IN JESUS'S NAME, *Amen.*

Share Your Story

PROMPT: When you reflect on your connection with your church community, what is one specific barrier you consistently face? On the other hand, what has been the most meaningful or unexpected moment of genuine connection you've experienced?

ACTION STEP: Thinking about your biggest hurdle to connecting, what is one small, manageable step you could take this week to overcome it? What is a recent moment of positive connection you've experienced, and how can you intentionally build on that this week?

FOR LOVED ONES AND CAREGIVERS: Given the realities of time, energy, and support, what is one specific way you have found to connect with your church family? What is one tangible, nondemanding way your church family could come alongside you this week to offer encouragement or support?

FOR PASTORS AND CHURCH LEADERS: What are some of the most effective and creative ways your church intentionally fosters a culture of genuine connection and integration for individuals with disabilities, their loved ones, and caregivers? What is one new, practical step your leadership team is considering to further break down barriers and build a more inclusive community?

DAY 27

Forging New Paths

LIVING AS A NEW CREATION

The Spirit of the Lord is upon me, because he has anointed me to proclaim good news to the poor. He has sent me to proclaim liberty to the captives and recovering of sight to the blind, to set at liberty those who are oppressed, to proclaim the year of the Lord's favor.

Luke 4:18–19

ALTHOUGH THE WORDS of Luke 4:18–19 first appear in Isaiah, Jesus's reading of them in the synagogue speaks to me most powerfully. The scene comes after Jesus was filled with the Holy Spirit and tempted in the wilderness. Jesus opened the scroll, read this passage, and then stopped at the word "favor." Then, he explained, "Today this Scripture has been fulfilled in your hearing" (Luke 4:21).

In a fallen world, where brokenness abounds due to sin, Jesus brought spiritual healing. It's worth noting that healing doesn't always equate to a cure. A cure often refers to the complete elimination of an illness, disease, or hurt so that no scars remain. Conversely, healing is a much broader concept that communicates restoring balance and wholeness. The process can involve recovery, repair, adaptation, or growth, even if the underlying condition doesn't completely disappear.

So whether you feel broken by addiction, abuse, fear, poverty, unforgiveness, or social injustice, know that Jesus came to heal and restore you. He proclaimed freedom for the spiritual captive—not by abolishing the law but by completely fulfilling it and offering life under grace.

Jesus also spoke to those who were "poor in spirit"—those who recognized their spiritual emptiness and need for God. For them, he offered an eternal, "imperishable, undefiled, and unfading" inheritance (1 Peter 1:4). Where sin had clouded their spiritual sight, he brought clarity. Many of the spiritually "blind" who had once focused on fulfilling the law's requirements were able to acknowledge him as Lord.

While Jesus performed many miracles that removed disease, disability, and physical illness, he consistently spoke of a deeper, more comprehensive healing beyond mere physical change. It encompassed:

- **BRIDGING THE CHASM** created by sin;
- **OFFERING FREEDOM** from striving for salvation through law;
- **FINDING CONTENTMENT** and meaning regardless of external circumstances; and
- **BEING BROUGHT INTO** the body of Christ, the church.

Jesus's teachings illustrated that wholeness and healing were not simply physical changes, but a change in heart and mind. These changes could only come through faith in Jesus. The amazing thing is, that same power is available to you today. You don't need a special ritual or a perfect life; all you have to do is simply invite Jesus into your heart. This invitation opens the door to a relationship that brings peace, hope, and true completeness.

If you're already a follower of Jesus, you understand this journey of faith isn't a one-time event. It's a continuous process of deepening your relationship with him and allowing his work in your life. Like any relationship, the bond of friendship strengthens as you spend time together.

So, what does spending time with Jesus look like?

It can include reading and meditating on God's Word, allowing the Holy Spirit to illuminate areas of your heart and mind that need to realign with Scripture. Growth can also come through prayer and spending time with other believers in Christ. It may be helpful to think of your prayer time as more of a conversation than an opportunity to present a list of requests. Spend time listening for guidance and encouragement, be honest about your struggles, and thank God for all he has done. As a follower of Christ, you are part of the body of Christ. Part of growing as a believer means spending time with other believers. Your particular gifts, words of encouragement, and wisdom can be used to encourage those around you.

Make no mistake—being a follower of Jesus won't make all your troubles disappear instantly. It won't fill your bank account, grant you that long-awaited dream vacation, dissolve discrimination, remove ableism, or erase hurt. It won't "fix" everything, whether inside or outside the church. What it will give you is something that can't be taken away: eternal life with Jesus, free from pain, sickness, disease, and disability.

While we wait for the complete fulfillment of that promise, he promises that, in him, we can have right now:

- **PEACE THAT DEFIES** even our greatest understanding (Philippians 4:7).
- **FRIENDSHIP, COMPANIONSHIP,** and love from One who has experienced the worst parts of us, yet will never disappoint, betray, or desert us (Romans 8:38–39).
- **HELP THAT ANSWERS** before we finish asking (Isaiah 65:24).
- **COURAGE TO FACE EVERY BATTLE,** and strength to continue when the nights are long (Isaiah 41:10).
- **LOVE THAT DOESN'T SIMPLY** avoid excluding us but actively invites us in (Luke 14:21, Matthew 18:12).

As we navigate this broken world, let's remind ourselves that Jesus has paid the price for our spiritual freedom and reconciliation to God. This truth gives us peace that passes all understanding, hope that does not fade, comfort that soothes our deepest hurts, and joy eternal. And God invites us to join him in sharing this truth with the world.

LORD, *I am amazed by your revolutionary love. Thank you for reconciling us to God and restoring what sin had stolen. Thank you for fulfilling the law, paying the ultimate penalty for our sin, and offering us life under grace. Lord, for those who have not yet invited you into their heart, give them courage to trust you. Help us grasp the depth of your love and let us live with a new sense of spiritual freedom.*

IN JESUS'S NAME, *Amen.*

Share Your Story

PROMPT: Identify one specific area of your life where you've experienced profound brokenness or hurt. How does the message of Jesus as the Anointed One, sent to bind up the brokenhearted (Isaiah 61:1), directly minister to that unique wound? Be specific about how his mission gives you hope.

ACTION STEP: Envision what wholeness would look like in that specific area of brokenness. What is one practical, tangible step you can take this week to intentionally invite Jesus into that journey of healing?

FOR LOVED ONES AND CAREGIVERS: In what specific ways does Jesus's mission to bind up the brokenhearted give you strength and encouragement in your caregiving role? As you reflect on his example of compassionate presence and love, what is one practical way you can demonstrate this to your loved one or client this week?

FOR PASTORS AND CHURCH LEADERS: Considering the mission of Jesus in Luke 4:18–19, in what specific ways is your church already embodying this message of freedom and healing for people with disabilities, their loved ones, and caregivers? What is one tangible, new initiative you can implement in the next month to more deeply live out this mission in your community?

DAY 28

Cultivating Gratitude

ACKNOWLEDGING PROGRESS

I will give thanks to the LORD with my whole heart; I will recount all of your wonderful deeds. I will be glad and exult in you; I will sing praise to your name, O Most High.

Psalm 9:1–2

"ASHER, what's one thing you're grateful for today?" asked Mathew.

It was the early days of my stepson's return home from residential treatment, and we had made gratitude a regular part of our day. It served as an opportunity to recognize large and small wins and blessings.

"I'm thankful that I can shower longer than five minutes," responded Asher, subtly making the distinction between being home versus in treatment.

Mathew looked at me. "Honey, how about you?"

"I'm thankful it's almost the weekend. One more day!" I said with a wide smile.

"And I'm thankful for our animals," shared Mathew, referring to our two cats and my service dog, Watson.

Mathew is a glass-half-full kind of man. I am, on the other hand, a glass-half-empty kind of woman. Neither perspective is better nor worse. Each of us is simply wired that way. Whether you're a glass-half-full kind of person or a glass-half-empty champion, rest assured: The world and the church need both types of people.

Many studies have documented gratitude's positive impact on mental and physical health. Gratitude supports heart health, reduces stress, improves sleep, strengthens the immune system, and lowers mortality.[32, 33] There are countless ways of practicing thankfulness: keeping a gratitude journal, saying a specific thank you, redirecting your thoughts, and expressing your gratitude toward others.

But if gratitude is so beneficial, should you continually express gratitude and suppress hardship and pain—as in "I'm sorry to hear about the loss of your leg, but you should be grateful you're still alive"? No! There can be too much of a good thing.

This type of forced gratitude, also known as toxic gratitude or positive mindfulness, leads to resentment and disillusionment. It keeps us from feeling or expressing negative emotions around difficult circumstances, which can lead to long-term trauma. Signs that you may be the recipient of toxic positivity include statements that make you feel guilty, ashamed, or afraid to show your real feelings.[34] On a systemic level, such thinking (*Things could be worse.*) makes us reluctant to advocate for change.

So how can we reconcile difficult seasons with Scripture that commands thankfulness in all circumstances (e.g., 1 Thessalonians 5:18)? How can we be grateful for all the growth we've experienced and the progress we've made when we still falter or our bodies still fail us? Blogger and Bible teacher Andrew Menkis offered this helpful insight: "Thankfulness isn't a key to getting rid of negativity, it is the path through those feelings."[35] He wrote, "Biblical positivity, or thankfulness, leads us to God in worship. . . . It allows us to be realistic and honest about our pain, while also finding hope and healing in Christ."[36]

We see this in Psalm 9, as David praised the Lord, amid his struggles. Even though the Psalm opened with praise (verses 1–2), David clearly faced danger and hardship. He reminded himself and God in Psalm 9:12, "he does not forget the cry of the afflicted." And in verse 13,

Avoiding Toxic Positivity

If you want to show your support to a friend or family member who is facing a difficult season, but you're afraid even your most genuine sentiment could be perceived as toxic positivity, consider these strategies that can help you meaningfully convey your support:

- Ask how you can help.
- Acknowledge the hard reality.
- Listen first.
- Remind them there's nothing wrong with not being okay.

he says, "See my affliction from those who hate me, O you who lift me up from the gates of death." David certainly understood the complexity of life and emotion. In the same way, we may celebrate progress and spiritual growth while fixing our eyes and heart on the Lord and trusting him amid heartache and difficulty.

As we see from the example of David, God's Word does not dismiss your challenges, but rather it demonstrates that moving forward requires walking through lament to gratitude. It means recalling the Lord's kindness and generosity toward you and remembering his character. It involves acknowledging reality, while giving yourself space to experience all your feelings. It means extending understanding to yourself but also recognizing that your experiences are not uncommon. All emotions, including sadness, are part of life. Don't give into the lie that tempts you to isolate. The Lord invites us to come to him with our "whole heart." He desires that nothing in our hearts be kept from him. So when you are struggling or sad, you can bring that part of your heart to him.

Victories in the arena of gratitude and honesty before God do not have to be monumental. As Zechariah 4:10 (NLT) says, "Do not despise these small beginnings, for the LORD rejoices to see the work begin." Think of David saying, "I will be glad and exult in you." Even in his grief or pain, when he maybe didn't have much to be grateful for, David knew he could lean on God's strength and nearness. He could still be honest with God about his suffering. After all, genuine gratitude doesn't sugarcoat painful experiences. But in the very next breath, he could praise God for his steadfast faithfulness.

The same is true for you. You might celebrate the honing of a new skill even as you experience no change or even setbacks on your disability journey. God wants you to come to him with all of it, the wonderful and the hard. You can practice gratitude while still acknowledging the hard. So whether you have a lot or only a little to be grateful for today, start with some small beginnings. Open your heart to God, who rejoices with you as you begin the work.

LORD, *thank you for rejoicing in small beginnings. Thank you for the victories that I've had up to this point. They are truly evidence of your grace in my life. Please protect my mind and my heart from the lies that seek to discourage me for my lack of progress. Open my eyes to the wins—small or big—that I have experienced, and teach me to cultivate a posture and mindset of genuine gratitude for the ways you have worked and continue to work in my life. Remind me that your work in my life will not end until I am with you. Encourage my heart today, and give me the desire, courage, and strength to persevere.*

IN JESUS'S NAME, *Amen.*

Share Your Story

PROMPT: Which way does your natural disposition tend to lean—toward hope or toward lament? Describe a time when your perspective shifted from one to the other, and what caused that change.

ACTION STEP: This week, write your own psalm that moves from a place of honest lament to a place of gratitude. Start by pouring out your genuine feelings of pain or struggle, then intentionally shift to thanking God for his faithfulness, even in the midst of hardship.

FOR LOVED ONES AND CAREGIVERS: Given the emotional and physical demands of your role, what is one specific thought pattern that makes practicing gratitude a struggle for you? What is one tangible strategy you will use today to intentionally redirect your thoughts toward gratitude?

FOR PASTORS AND CHURCH LEADERS: In what specific ways are you and your leadership team intentionally demonstrating biblical positivity—which embraces both lament and hope—to your church family? How are you actively training your ministry teams and staff to avoid toxic positivity and instead create a safe space for people to express their honest struggles? What is one change you could make to better equip them for this?

DAY 29

Pursuing God-Sized Dreams

HIS GOOD PLANS FOR YOU

For we are his workmanship,
created in Christ Jesus for good works,
which God prepared beforehand,
that we should walk in them.

Ephesians 2:10

MATHEW AND I had been married less than three weeks when he suggested we take a quick trip from Maryland to Florida. We had been discussing a potential move to South Florida for two primary reasons: the warmer weather and Mathew's work in addiction recovery. (South Florida has the infamous distinction of being the addiction recovery capital of the United States.) Given that we were in the throes of a Maryland winter, I wasted no time looking for flights.

My desire to relocate to a warmer climate first began several years prior to meeting Mathew. I had scouted out several areas and taken weekend trips with friends. I even applied for several jobs in Southern states, but the Lord had closed every door. Given my previously unsuccessful efforts to move, I secretly doubted that our joint desire to move would come to fruition.

But less than two months after our initial trip to South Florida, we packed our bags, loaded the moving truck, and headed to Wellington, Florida. As it turned out, my desire to move to a warmer climate as a single woman wasn't bad or wrong. My timing simply differed from God's. Truth be told, I'm not always happy with his plans in the moment. But—in the end—I invariably recognize that his plans and his timing are far better than I could have dreamed.

Proverbs 19:21 speaks in part to this idea, saying, "Many are the plans in the mind of a man, but it is the purpose of the LORD that will stand." If you only looked at Proverbs 19:21, you may come away wrongly thinking that God's primary response to your plans is like that of a domineering father who overrides plans simply because he can. But that image couldn't be further from the truth.

As you consider the plans and dreams in your heart, you may feel eager, excited, anxious, fearful—and maybe even a bit angry—as you see others receive what you want. You may be thinking, *If God has good works prepared for me, then why don't I have what I've always wanted? Why does my neighbor always seem to get what I want? God knows I want nothing more than to have a child. Isn't that a good desire?*

Friend, the Lord understands your mixed emotions. We are invited to bring all these feelings and dreams to the Lord and lay them at his feet. As you seek him and his wisdom—and not simply his blessings—he will align your heart with his, "and he will give you the desires of your heart" (Psalm 37:4). Ephesians 2:10 reveals God's interest and involvement in your life plans and shows his character more clearly: a loving, caring, generous, and good Father.

According to Psalm 139:16–17, God saw you as "unformed substance" and planned your days before laying the foundation of the world. Like an excited and eager first-time parent, even before you were formed, God began dreaming of adventures with you. It's not as if he made you, then scrambled to find good works for you to do. Quite the opposite, as a matter of fact. Out of his specific love for you, he prepared a plan for you. You are his workmanship. You reflect your maker's wisdom, creativity, skill, and love. The same Creator who made each star in the night sky created you and the work intended for you in this life.

Even more wonderful, he did not create you simply to be a decorative piece in the universe. According to 2 Corinthians 5:17–18, "if anyone is in Christ, he is a new creation. The old has passed away; behold, the new has come. All this is from God, who through Christ reconciled us to himself." In other words, he made a way for you to be in relationship with him and join his mission. He imparted to you specific skills and abilities and gave you a unique love for things like art, music, science, math, or writing.

These divinely given passions can leave us eager to dive headfirst into "dreaming big for God." But the Bible cautions us against making assumptions about future plans, saying in James 4:13 (NIV), "Now listen, you who say, 'Today or tomorrow we will go to this or that city, spend a year there, carry on business and make money.'" Making plans and having dreams is good and part of God's design for us, but we should be careful about becoming boastful about our futures or clinging too hard to control. After all, in the grand scheme of eternity, our lives are like tiny water droplets, disappearing quickly.

In light of all of this, you may be wondering how you can be certain of God's plans for you. Thankfully, the Lord does not play hide and seek when it comes to his plans. There's no cosmic riddle to solve. Psalm 37 provides some good parameters to keep in mind:

- **DON'T WORRY:** Seeing others get what you hoped for—through their own efforts or dishonest means—can be difficult, but it's important to remember that your story is your own and won't be the same as anyone else's. Trust that God has unique and good plans just for you.

- **TRUST THE LORD:** You can choose to trust in your own efforts or give your plans to the Lord, who has infinitely more power and wisdom. Trusting the Lord is always the better option, even though it may mean your dreams go unfulfilled.

- **DO GOOD:** Unfulfilled dreams can lead to sadness, anger, and envy, especially when you see others succeeding and obtaining what they desire, even if it's through dishonesty. But don't give in to the temptation to do harm or pursue dishonest gain all in the name of "dreaming big for God." Focus on the good.

DWELL IN THE LAND: Unless the Lord has "opened the door" on an opportunity or confirmed a particular direction to go, consider staying where you are for now. Ask the Lord to help you "be still" and "wait patiently for him."

BEFRIEND FAITHFULNESS: Invite faithfulness to be your companion as you wait on the Lord. Ask the Lord to help you better understand what it looks like to be faithful in your current season.

DELIGHT YOURSELF IN THE LORD: This refers to more than simply white-knuckling on joy in the Lord. It refers to spending time with God through prayer and worship, which will give you a deeper understanding of his love and character.

LORD, *thank you for the dreams and plans in my heart. Please help me discern what is from you and what I have pursued in my own strength. I want to follow you and trust your ways. But some of the dreams have been on my heart a very long time. I've felt myself becoming anxious, envious, and at times angry that they remain unfulfilled. Sometimes you answer my prayers differently than I expect. To be honest, it frustrates me. In the end, though, I'm thankful that your plans are far better than my own—and that you've been dreaming about the things that we'll do together since before I was even born. Lord, I need your help. I want to trust you and be patient. I want your desires to be my desires.*

IN JESUS'S NAME, *Amen.*

Share Your Story

PROMPT: What is one dream God has placed on your heart? How does this dream align with your gifts, passions, and the needs you see in the world?

ACTION STEP: Take time to journal about your dream. What is one specific, prayerful step you've already taken, and what is one new step you can take this week? What have you felt the Lord telling you about this dream, and how has that influenced your actions?

FOR LOVED ONES AND CAREGIVERS: What is one dream you've had to put on hold due to your caregiving responsibilities? What is one small, tangible way you could begin to reconnect with that dream? How can you specifically ask the Lord for guidance in finding a balance between your responsibilities and your desires?

FOR PASTORS AND CHURCH LEADERS: What is one dream God has placed on your heart for your own life and leadership? What is one specific dream you have for your congregation, particularly for people with disabilities, their loved ones, and caregivers? What is one tangible, new step you can take this month to begin moving toward that dream?

DAY 30

A Life of Purpose

LIVING FULLY AND FREELY

The thief comes only to steal and kill and destroy.
I came that they may have life and have it abundantly.

John 10:10

AS WE COME TO THE END of our journey, I would love to guarantee for you that everything will be easy and joyful from here. But you and I both know that's not possible. The reality of life this side of Heaven guarantees we will continue to face hardships and difficulties.

In the course of writing this devotional, my husband, Mathew, underwent multiple shoulder surgeries. The long-term prognosis still remains uncertain. But the Lord has met and blessed our family in unexpected ways in this difficult season. Mathew is fulfilling a lifelong dream to write music with dear friends—a reminder that joy and sadness coexist.

As for me, I've left my job after approximately twenty-two years, and I'm not entirely sure what's next. I'm eager to see what the Lord has in store. As a self-proclaimed Type A personality, I don't say that flippantly. Uncertainty typically causes me anxiety, so the Lord has most certainly been at work.

What about you? You may be looking at your life right now and wondering, *Where is the abundant life Jesus references in John 10:10?*

I offer this for your consideration: The abundant life Jesus promised is not simply at some unknown time in the future when we enter eternity. It is right here, right now. It is life with him at the center. It happened the moment you asked Jesus to be Lord of your life. And, if you haven't asked him yet, I invite you to do so right now. I assure you, he has been eagerly waiting for you.

As we close our time together, I want to remind you of the incredible truth of life with the Trinity. I hope you feel a renewed sense of purpose and meaning, knowing that God has had a plan for you from the very beginning. His greatest desire is to be in relationship with you, and through Jesus's sacrifice, you have been given the gift of the Holy Spirit. The Holy Spirit is your constant companion, here to help you understand and live out the unique purposes God has for your life.

Because of God's amazing love for you, you can experience love and connection with your heavenly Father that is unmatched by any human relationship. Jesus took on rejection so that you could have the privilege of connecting with the Father and with your brothers and sisters in Christ. You are now a vessel of that love, called to show and share it with a world that desperately needs it.

And in this life with God, fear and anxiety no longer control you. You can have a deep sense of peace and joy that is not dependent on your circumstances. Your trials, illnesses, and struggles are temporary. The enemy may try to steal, kill, and destroy, but Jesus has already overcome the grave. You can fix your eyes on the Author and Perfector of your faith, confident that true joy awaits you.

I know that not every dream will come true and that you will continue to face difficulties. But even in those moments, there is an opportunity for growth and maturity. You are being conformed into Christ's image, and that is a beautiful journey worth persevering through.

Finally, remember that God offers you wholeness and healing that go far beyond physical or cognitive ability. Jesus has satisfied your greatest need by paying the penalty for your sin, and you are completely forgiven and free. You are a beloved child in God's family, and your eternal home awaits you. This promise of a future without pain or sorrow can shape how you face every difficulty and illness in the present moment.

Dear friend, you serve a God of justice and mercy. Though the enemy may continue to cause you pain, you can rest securely in the arms of a Father who will see that justice is served and that all tears will be wiped away. God is with you, right here, right now. May you experience the fullness of his presence, his peace, his comfort, and his strength.

LORD, *thank you for being with my dear friend on this journey. Would you regularly remind them of the wisdom you've given them as they continue to see what it means to be divinely disabled. Thank you for your unwavering love, kindness, mercy, and grace. I know there will be trials ahead, but I pray they would take comfort in knowing that you will be with them. Bring them back to the words you've spoken to them on this journey as often as they need it. Thank you for all that you have done and are doing in their life, Lord.*

IN JESUS'S NAME, *Amen.*

Share Your Story

PROMPT: Of all the principles you've explored on this journey, what is one key principle you feel most compelled to carry forward? How will you intentionally integrate this principle into your daily life?

ACTION STEP: Thinking about the key principle you identified, what is one small, tangible action you will take today to put it into practice?

FOR LOVED ONES AND CAREGIVERS: What has been the most significant shift in your perspective since the start of this journey? What is one specific, manageable step you will take this week to live out this new perspective? Who is one person you can share this with for accountability?

FOR PASTORS AND CHURCH LEADERS: What is one new strategy you can implement to better equip your entire church family to live an abundant life with Christ? What is one specific, compassionate strategy you will implement to support those in a trial-filled season or those facing disability?

Studying the Landscape: A Brief Disability History Timeline

THIS TIMELINE HIGHLIGHTS key events, legislation, and Supreme Court interpretations shaping disability rights in the United States from the seventeenth century to the present day.[37, 38, 39]

Please note this timeline is not exhaustive and is for informational purposes only.

17TH–18TH CENTURIES: COLONIAL ERA AND ENLIGHTENMENT

EARLY COLONIAL VIEWS: Disability is often viewed through a religious lens, sometimes seen as punishment or a sign of evil. Societal responses vary from care within families to neglect and social exclusion.

ENLIGHTENMENT INFLUENCES: The emphasis on reason and individual rights begins to subtly shift perceptions, with some thinkers advocating for more humane treatment, although these ideas have limited practical impact on the lives of disabled individuals at the time.

19TH CENTURY: INSTITUTIONALIZATION AND EARLY ADVOCACY

EARLY 1800S: The establishment of the first residential schools for the deaf (American School for the Deaf, 1817) and the blind (Perkins School for the Blind, 1829) marks the beginning of formal education for some disabled individuals.

MID-1800S: The rise of large asylums for individuals with mental illness and intellectual disabilities leads to widespread institutionalization, often characterized by poor conditions and a lack of individualized care.

LATE 1800S: The "Ugly Laws" enacted in some cities prohibit people with visible disabilities from appearing in public, reflecting deep-seated societal stigma.

20TH CENTURY: CIVIL RIGHTS MOVEMENT AND LEGISLATIVE MILESTONES

EARLY 1900S: The Eugenics Movement gains traction, leading to the forced sterilization of individuals with disabilities in many states (Indiana's law in 1907). This practice is upheld by the Supreme Court in *Buck v. Bell* (1927).

1920: The Smith-Fess Act establishes vocational rehabilitation programs for disabled civilians.

1935: The Social Security Act provides some financial assistance to individuals with disabilities, though it has limited scope.

POST-WORLD WAR II: Disabled veterans returning from the war advocate for greater accessibility and rights, contributing to the growing Disability Rights Movement.

1950: The development of national barrier-free standards begins, driven by the efforts of disabled veterans and advocacy organizations.

1961: The American Standards Association publishes the first accessibility standards for buildings.

1964: The Civil Rights Act, while groundbreaking, does not explicitly include disability as a protected category.

1968: The Architectural Barriers Act requires federally funded buildings to be accessible.

1972: *PARC v. Pennsylvania* and *Mills v. Board of Education of District of Columbia* establish the right to education for children with disabilities.

1973: The Rehabilitation Act is a landmark achievement, prohibiting discrimination based on disability in federally funded programs and activities (Section 504). This act lays the groundwork for future disability rights legislation.

1975: The Education for All Handicapped Children Act (later amended to Individuals with Disabilities Education Act [IDEA]) mandates free and appropriate public education for children with disabilities in the least restrictive environment.

1977: Disability rights activists stage sit-ins at federal buildings to demand the implementation of Section 504 of the Rehabilitation Act.

1982: *Board of Education of Hendrick Hudson Central School District v. Rowley* provides the Supreme Court's first interpretation of "free appropriate public education" under IDEA, stating schools are not required to maximize each child's potential.

1984: The Voting Accessibility for the Elderly and Handicapped Act ensures accessibility at polling places.

1986: The Air Carrier Access Act prohibits discrimination by airlines against passengers with disabilities.

1988: Civil Rights Restoration Act of 1987: Enacted in March 1988 over a presidential veto, this act was a crucial victory for disability rights. It overturned the 1984 Supreme Court ruling in *Grove City College v. Bell*, which had narrowed the scope of civil rights laws. The Act clarified that if any part of an institution (like a university) receives federal funding, the *entire institution* must comply with anti-discrimination laws, including Section 504 of the Rehabilitation Act of 1973. This closed a major loophole and restored broad, institution-wide protections against disability discrimination in federally funded programs.

1988: Gallaudet is the only university in the world specifically for Deaf and hard-of-hearing students. In March 1988, the campus erupts in protest when the Board of Trustees selects Elisabeth Zinser, a hearing woman who does not know sign language, over two highly qualified Deaf candidates. Despite the University's 124-year history, it had never had a Deaf president. After eight days of national media coverage and marches to the U.S. Capitol, the Board concedes, appointing Dr. I. King Jordan as Gallaudet's first Deaf president. The Deaf President Now movement is widely credited with providing the political momentum needed to pass the Americans with Disabilities Act (ADA) in 1990. It shifts the public perception of disability from a "medical tragedy" to a "civil rights" issue.

1990: The Americans with Disabilities Act (ADA) is signed into law, a comprehensive civil rights law prohibiting discrimination based on disability in employment (Title I), state and local governments (Title II), public accommodations (Title III), telecommunications (Title IV), and miscellaneous (Title V).

1999: *Olmstead v. L.C.* holds that unjustified segregation of individuals with disabilities in institutions constitutes discrimination under the ADA, promoting community integration.

2001: *PGA Tour, Inc. v. Martin* rules that the ADA requires reasonable modifications to be made in professional sports to accommodate individuals with disabilities.

2002: The Help America Vote Act aims to make voting systems more accessible.

2008: The ADA Amendments Act (ADAAA) expands the definition of disability, making it easier for individuals to establish protection under the ADA, responding to Supreme Court interpretations that had narrowed its scope.

2010: The 21st Century Communications and Video Accessibility Act updates accessibility requirements for communication technologies.

2017: *Fry v. Napoleon Community Schools* clarifies when individuals with disabilities can pursue claims under the ADA without first exhausting administrative procedures under IDEA.

2022: *Cummings v. Premier Rehab Keller, PLLC* limits the remedies available under the Rehabilitation Act and the Affordable Care Act, ruling that emotional distress damages are not recoverable in private actions.

2025: The Supreme Court hears *A.J.T. v. Osseo Area Schools*, a case that expands a student's ability to sue for discrimination. The Supreme Court rules that students' families do not have to prove "bad faith or gross misconduct," which the court decides is too high a standard. It rules unanimously that "deliberate indifference," which is the typical standard for similar disability-related cases, is a sufficient standard.

Key Legislative Advancements

THE REHABILITATION ACT OF 1973

(SECTION 501): Requires federal agencies to implement action plans for the hiring, placement, and advancement of individuals with disabilities within the federal government. Effective January 3, 2018, federal agencies have a specific affirmative action obligation to provide Personal Assistance Services (PAS) to employees with targeted disabilities. This requirement is distinct from the obligation to provide reasonable accommodations.

(SECTION 503): Prohibits employment discrimination based on disability by federal contractors and subcontractors and requires them to take action to employ and advance qualified individuals with disabilities.

(SECTION 504): The first federal civil rights protection for people with disabilities, prohibiting discrimination in federally funded programs.

(SECTION 508): Requires federal agencies to make their electronic and information technology (EIT) accessible to people with disabilities, including websites, software, and electronic documents.

THE INDIVIDUALS WITH DISABILITIES EDUCATION ACT OF 1975 (IDEA)

Ensures that children with disabilities receive a free and appropriate public education in the least restrictive environment.

THE AIR CARRIER ACCESS ACT OF 1986 (ACAA)

Prohibits discrimination against passengers with disabilities by air carriers, ensuring equal access to air travel and related services.

THE AMERICANS WITH DISABILITIES ACT OF 1990 (ADA)

Extends civil rights protections to people with disabilities (and those who are associated with them) in various aspects of life, including employment, state and local government, public services, public accommodations, and telecommunications. This landmark law protects those with a history of impairment and those who may be perceived by others as having a disability.

THE TELECOMMUNICATIONS ACT OF 1996 (SECTION 255)

Requires telecommunications equipment and services to be accessible to people with disabilities, ensuring features like TTY compatibility, hearing aid compatibility, and access to visual information.

THE ADA AMENDMENTS ACT OF 2008 (ADAAA)

Broadens the definition of disability under the ADA, providing greater protection by focusing on whether discrimination occurred rather than the severity of the impairment.

THE WORKFORCE INNOVATION AND OPPORTUNITY ACT OF 2014 (WIOA)

Governs federal job training programs and emphasizes integrated employment for individuals with disabilities, promoting competitive, integrated employment and community-based services.

Taking in the Views: Models of Disability

How we understand and think about disability influences everything from government policy and professional practices (e.g., doctors or service providers) to societal attitudes and daily interactions with and by people with disabilities. Experts have identified anywhere from three to upward of twenty models to explain the various perspectives. Each model examines the origins and impact of disability on individuals, families, societies, and cultures through a distinct lens. But the concept of disability is not straightforward and cannot fit into rigid categories. Societal views and individual beliefs often blend multiple elements from different models.

While the social model has been particularly influential within the Disability Rights Movement, understanding the spectrum of models can be helpful. Some prominent models include:

THE MORAL MODEL interprets disability as resulting from sin, moral failing, or supernatural forces, finding its roots in ancient religious or cultural beliefs.

THE MEDICAL MODEL defines disability as an individual medical problem caused by disease or injury, focusing on diagnosis, treatment, and cure (i.e., removal of any sign of illness or disease) by professionals.

THE SOCIAL MODEL attributes disability challenges to society's lack of accommodation for a disability or accessibility.

THE BIOPSYCHOSOCIAL MODEL takes a holistic view of disability, seeing it as an interaction between health conditions, personal factors, and environmental factors.

THE CULTURAL MODEL emphasizes the various definitions and experiences of disability across cultures and highlights the need for cultural sensitivity.

THE PSYCHOLOGICAL MODEL centers on the individual's psychological and emotional response to disability and focuses on adaptation and coping.

THE CHARITY MODEL views people with disabilities and their circumstances as heartbreaking and deserving of sympathy and kindness, which can foster dependency.

Notes

INTRODUCTION: PREPARING FOR THE JOURNEY

1 "Cerebral Palsy Statistics," Cerebral Palsy Guide, accessed April 18, 2025, https://www.cerebralpalsyguide.com/cerebral-palsy/statistics/.

2 The term "activities of daily living" (ADLs), also known as basic activities of daily living (BADLs), refers to activities such as walking, feeding, dressing and grooming, toileting, bathing, and transferring. Individual needs vary from very little assistance to full dependence. The term "instrumental activities of daily living" (IADLs) are tasks learned in early adulthood, requiring more complex thinking and organizational skills. This term typically refers to managing tasks such as finances, transportation, shopping and meal preparation, housecleaning and basic maintenance, communications (e.g., phone and email), and medication.

3 "Factsheet on Persons with Disabilities," United Nations, Department of Economic and Social Affairs, accessed April 16, 2025, https://www.un.org/development/desa/disabilities/resources/factsheet-on-persons-with-disabilities.html.

4 Chris Woznicki, "'Disability and the Church': A Few Takeaways," *CWoznicki Think Out Loud* (blog), July 28, 2021, https://cwoznicki.com/2021/07/28/disability-and-the-church-a-few-takeaways/.

5 "CDC Data Shows Over 70 Million U.S. Adults Reported Having a Disability," Centers for Disease Control and Prevention, July 16, 2024, https://www.cdc.gov/media/releases/2024/s0716-Adult-disability.html.

6 "CDC and Disability and Health," Centers for Disease Control and Prevention, April 7, 2025, https://www.cdc.gov/disability-and-health/articles-documents/mental-health-of-people-with-disabilities.html.

7 Daniel H. Gillison, "The Intersection of Faith and Mental Health," NAMI: National Alliance on Mental Illness, August 19, 2022, https://www.nami.org/Blogs/From-the-CEO/August-2022/The-Intersection-of-Faith-and-Mental-Health.

8 *Standing Up and Stepping In: Guardian's 12th Annual Workplace Benefits Study*, Guardian Group Benefits, December 15, 2023, https://connect.guardiangroupbenefits.com/l/503851/2023-12-15/6yw1b6/503851/1702675399bBkGiG78/Guardian_12th_Annual_WBS_Standing_Up_and_Stepping_In_1215.pdf.

9 "37.1 million people provided unpaid eldercare in 2021–2022," *The Economics Daily*, Bureau of Labor Statistics, U.S. Department of Labor, October 2, 2023, https://www.bls.gov/opub/ted/2023/37-1-million-people-provided-unpaid-eldercare-in-2021-2022.htm.

10 U.S. Department of Labor, "37.1 Million People Provided Unpaid Eldercare."

11 "Why People with Disabilities Are Siloed in the Church (and How to Change That)," Joni & Friends, September 22, 2023, https://joniandfriends.org/for-the-church/why-people-with-disabilities-are-siloed-in-the-church-and-how-to-change-that/.

12 Sandra Peoples, "Why I'm Hopeful for the Future of Disability Ministry," The Gospel Coalition, January 10, 2024, https://www.thegospelcoalition.org/article/hopeful-disability-ministry/.

13 Stephen Grcevich, "What Are the Stats on Disability and Church?" Church4EveryChild, February 9, 2016, https://church4everychild.org/2016/02/09/what-are-the-stats-on-disability-and-church/.

14 Grcevich, "What Are the Stats."

15 C. Trent Broussard, "Including Disabled in the Church: More Than a Ramp," *Artistic Theologian,* May 8, 2020, https://equipthecalled.com/at-article/including-disabled-in-the-church-more-than-a-ramp/.

16 Gerry Hendershot, "A Statistical Note on the Religiosity of Persons with Disabilities," *Disability Studies Quarterly* 26, no. 4 (2006), https://doi.org/10.18061/dsq.v26i4.813.

17 David R. Hodge and Conroy Reynolds, "Spirituality Among People with Disabilities: A Nationally Representative Study of Spiritual and Religious Profiles," *Health & Social Work* 44, no. 2 (May 2019): 75–86, https://doi.org/10.1093/hsw/hly035.

DAY 2: FORLORN BUT NOT FORSAKEN: GOD SEES YOU

18 "129. Connect Deeply: How to Communicate So People Feel Seen and Heard," Stanford Graduate School of Business, posted February 13, 2024, YouTube, http://www.youtube.com/watch?v=8vxyECzruUU.

19 Matthew Henry, *Matthew Henry's Commentary on the Whole Bible: Complete and Unabridged in One Volume* (Hendrickson, 1994), John 9. Logos Research edition.

DAY 3: CALLING FOR HELP: SEEKING ANSWERS IN THE DARKNESS

20 Britt Merrick, "When Sparrows Fall," posted 2013, Vimeo, 54:40, https://vimeo.com/groups/65464/videos/58318290.

DAY 4: WHEN HOPES GO UNFULFILLED: UNMET EXPECTATIONS

21 Thomas E. Reynolds, "The Cult of Normalcy," *Christian Reflection,* Disability issue (2022): 25, 30, https://ifl.web.baylor.edu/sites/g/files/ecbvkj771/files/2022-12/Disability.pdf.

DAY 6: ALL HOPE IS NOT LOST: RECOGNIZING DIVINE PRESENCE

22 “The Meal,” Bible Hub, accessed April 22, 2025, https://biblehub.com/topical/t/the_meal.htm.

DAY 8: GOD MAKES NO MISTAKES: YOU ARE HIS MASTERPIECE

23 Hannah Ashworth, “How Long Is Your DNA?” BBC Science Focus, https://www.sciencefocus.com/the-human-body/how-long-is-your-dna.

24 “12 Facts at 12 Weeks,” Charlotte Lozier Institute, April 25, 2023, https://lozierinstitute.org/12-facts-at-12-weeks/.

DAY 9: STRENGTHEN YOUR INNER BEING: ASKING FOR HOLY SPIRIT POWER

25 Andrew Murray, *Humility: The Journey Toward Holiness* (Bethany House, 2001), 41.

DAY 11: BEING COURAGEOUS: REFLECTING DIVINE COMPANIONSHIP

26 Nadia Ibrahim,“Model: Nadia Ibrahim,” Bold Beauty Project, https://www.boldbeautyproject.com/portfolio-items/nadia-ibrahim/.

DAY 12: PURSUING JUSTICE: IDENTIFYING INEQUITIES

27 Johnny Payne, “The American Church and the Americans with Disabilities Act,” *Journal of Religion & Society* 23 (2021), https://cdr.creighton.edu/server/api/core/bitstreams/b23248c4-789a-452d-b69b-36638e79ec4f/content.

DAY 18: HOPE IN THE WAITING: TRUSTING GOD'S TIMING

28 Madeline Crowley, "Disability History: The 1977 504 Sit-In," Disability Rights Florida, April 4, 2023, https://disabilityrightsflorida.org/blog/entry/504-sit-in-history.

DAY 21: EXPERIENCING JOY ON THE JOURNEY: CULTIVATING GRATITUDE IN UNCERTAINTY

29 Jayshree Ochwani, "Negativity Bias: Meaning, Psychology, and Examples," Octet Design Journal, April 28, 2025, https://octet.design/journal/negativity-bias/.

DAY 22: INVITING OTHERS INTO YOUR STORY: BEING VULNERABLE

30 "Health Effects of Social Isolation and Loneliness," Centers for Disease Control and Prevention, Social Connection, May 15, 2024, https://www.cdc.gov/social-connectedness/risk-factors/index.html#cdc_risk_factors_other_factor-risk-factors-for-individuals-and-groups.

31 Zara Abrams, "The Science of Why Friendships Keep Us Healthy," *Monitor on Psychology* 54, no. 4 (June 2023), https://www.apa.org/monitor/2023/06/cover-story-science-friendship.

DAY 28: CULTIVATING GRATITUDE: ACKNOWLEDGING PROGRESS

32 Nicole McDermott, "The Mental Health Benefits of Gratitude," Forbes Health, November 10, 2023, https://www.forbes.com/health/mind/mental-health-benefits-of-gratitude/.

33 Maureen Salamon, "Gratitude Enhances Health, Brings Happiness—and May Even Lengthen Lives," Harvard Health Publishing, September 11, 2024, https://www.health.harvard.edu/blog/gratitude-enhances-health-brings-happiness-and-may-even-lengthen-lives-202409113071.

34 Kendra Cherry, "Why Toxic Positivity Can Be Harmful," Verywell Mind, May 14, 2024, https://www.verywellmind.com/what-is-toxic-positivity-5093958.

35 Andrew Menkis, "When Giving Thanks Becomes Toxic," Core Christianity, November 23, 2021, https://corechristianity.com/resources/articles/when-giving-thanks-becomes-toxic.

36 Menkis, "When Giving Thanks Becomes Toxic."

STUDYING THE LANDSCAPE: A BRIEF DISABILITY HISTORY TIMELINE

37 "Disability Rights Timeline," Temple University Institute on Disabilities, https://disabilities.temple.edu/resources/disability-rights-timeline.

38 "Timeline of Disability Rights in the United States," Wikipedia, last modified April 21, 2025, https://en.wikipedia.org/wiki/Timeline_of_disability_rights_in_the_United_States.

39 "Timeline of Disability Rights in the United States," Accessibility.com, July 26, 2020, https://www.accessibility.com/resources/timeline-of-disability-rights.

About the Author

Nadia Ibrahim Mossburg, born with cerebral palsy, uses her writing to navigate challenges and advocate for others in the disability community. With degrees in English, journalism, and social work, in addition to her experience as a senior adviser in disability policy, she has been a driving force for over two decades in improving disability policy—at the national, state, and local levels—advancing greater equity, and advocating for better employment, emergency management, public health, and public transportation. Over the last thirty-seven years, she has also led Bible studies and served on many teams at her church.

Nadia and her husband, Mathew, live in the Nashville area with their three cats, Toulouse, Gary, and Bo, who love their brother Watson, Nadia's third service dog, who is enjoying retirement.